UVEITIS

Symposium of Papers read before the Ophthalmological Section of the American Medical Association, at the annual meeting, Saratoga, N.Y., June, 1902

"Concerning the Symptomatology and Etiology of Certain Types of Uveitis."
G. E. DE SCHWEINITZ, A.M., M.D., Philadelphia

"Analysis of Thirty-seven Cases of Uveitis."
HIRAM WOODS, M.D., Baltimore

"The Diagnostic Importance of Keratitis Punctata Interna (Descemetitis)."
HARRY FRIEDENWALD, A.B., M.D., Baltimore

"Injuries of the Eye Productive of Disease of the Uveal Tract." HOWARD F. HANSELL, M.D., Philadelphia

"Pathology of Uveitis."
WILLIAM H. WILDER, M.D., Chicago

"The Treatment of Certain Non-Specific Lesions of the Uveal Tract with Pilocarpin and Sweat Baths."
THOMAS A. WOODRUFF, M.D., Chicago

"The Treatment of Uveitis."
WILBUR B. MARPLE, M.D., New York City

CHICAGO:
AMERICAN MEDICAL ASSOCIATION PRESS
1902

CONCERNING THE SYMPTOMATOLOGY AND ETIOLOGY OF CERTAIN TYPES OF UVEITIS.

G. E. DE SCHWEINITZ, A.M., M.D.

PHILADELPHIA.

In ophthalmic practice three disease manifestations are encountered to which the name "keratitis punctata" has been applied. Two of these are affections of the cornea, the third is not; that is to say, the primary lesion is not corneal. They are as follows: (a) *keratitis superficialis punctata,* in which, in general terms, numerous small punctiform or linear spots appear below Bowman's membrane, the overlying cornea being slightly hazy and the epithelium a little elevated; (b) *keratitis punctata vera* or *syphilitica* of Mauthner, in which circumscribed pinhead-sized, grayish spots appear in the parenchyma of the cornea, and, moreover, in its various layers; the iris is not involved. Constitutional syphilis is the etiologic factor. To distinguish it from the preceding manifestations Fuchs suggests the name "keratitis punctata profunda." (c) *Keratitis punctata,* in which a notable manifestation consists of a precipitate of opaque dots on the posterior elastic lamina of the cornea, generally arranged in a triangular manner, with apex pointing upward, and which from the beginning may be or may not be associated with the signs of iritis.

To this last-named condition the older writers gave the names "aquo-capsulitis" and "hydro-meningitis," because it was believed that it represented a disease depending on an inflammation of a hyaloid membrane, which was supposed to line the anterior and posterior chambers as a serous sac and which was connected with the hyaloid of the vitreous.

With the belief that the disease depended on a specific participation of the membrane of Descemet in its lesions, arose the name "descemetitis," which is still commonly employed.

To those cases in which this punctate deposit on the posterior lamina of the cornea is associated with an iritis, without great tendency to form synechiæ, with a deep anterior chamber and with a disposition to increased intraocular tension, the name "serous iritis" has been and is still commonly given, but, as De Wecker very forcibly objects, the inflammatory products of a serous iritis is not of a serous nature, but is essentially cellular. The iris suffers secondarily from this cellular infiltration which is communicated to all the neighboring parts, the sclerotic, the cornea and the choroid. The points of departure of this cellular inundation are the lymphatic spaces of the eye, and he contends, therefore, that a serous iritis represents a lymphangitis anterior of the eye, having its principal situation in the pericorneal lymph spaces.

Long ago Von Arlt noted that in a certain number of eyes with punctate deposits on the cornea inflammatory changes in the iris are practically absent and the pupil dilates readily. These cases he attributed entirely to cyclitis. The cyclitic origin of the disease has been strongly maintained by E. Treacher Collins, especially after his discovery of the glands of the ciliary body, his belief being that the so-called serous iritis is primarily a catarrhal inflammation of these glands. The secretion of these glands, he maintains, becomes augmented, causing increase in the aqueous humor and deepening of the anterior chamber. The aqueous becomes altered in character, contains leucocytes, pigment cells and fibrin, and these formed elements gravitate and are deposited on the lower portion of the posterior face of the cornea. Therefore, it has been suggested that the disease should be named "serous cyclitis," or "iridocyclitis."

It has, however, been noticed by many that when the characteristic punctate deposits appear upon the posterior surface of the cornea, if the media are sufficiently. clear, recent patches of choroiditis can often, perhaps always, be found in some portion of the fundus. Particularly good studies of this association have been made in England. beginning, I think, with Hill Griffith's observations more than fifteen years ago. He believed that the dots on Descemet's membrane were formed in the choroid, set free in the vitreous and carried by the nutrient currents of the eye to be deposited on the back of the cornea. His view necessitated the admission that the suspensory ligament was permeable to solid particles. The choroidal origin of so-called descemetitis, however, is much older than this. For example, Von Graefe himself described in 1856 the association of choroidal lesions with this condition, and we find Schweigger stating that inasmuch as the ligamentum pectinatum sinks into the anterior part of the ciliary body, it may be easily understood how the epithelium upon the membrane of Descemet may become affected by an extension of disease from the choroid without any participation by the iris, and he goes on to describe a case in point, the choroidal disease having been situated in the macular region. I mention these facts because quite recently a good deal has been written on this subject as if the association of this condition with choroidal disease was a new discovery.

It is well known that not only in so-called serous iritis, but in all varieties of iritis, corneal lesions are always demonstrable by careful examination with a suitable corneal loup in the form of infiltrations in the substantia propria, dot-like deposits on Descemet's membrane, and striations in the posterior corneal layers. These have been well described and classified by Dr. H. Friedenwald. There is, however, one fairly constant clinical picture, which is, in a sense, characteristic, to which the names previously recited, all of which are more or less inexact and misleading, have been applied, viz., a deposit of variously-sized and colored dots, arranged usually in a triangular manner on the posterior layer of the cornea; an anterior chamber, sometimes deep and sometimes of ordinary depth; generally, but not constantly, iritis and cyclitis; hyalitis, and practically always some form of choroiditis, the last-named conditions being the primary lesions in most of the cases. In perfect examples there is reason to believe that the entire uveal tract is more or less involved, and hence the name uveitis is appropriate.

In general terms, the causes of uveitis may be diathetic, toxic or infectious. Thus we have causes depending on certain constitutional diseases, for example, rheumatism, gout and diabetes; on specific infectious diseases, for example, influenza, syphilis, gonorrhea, tuberculosis and scrofula, that is, tuberculosis of the lymph glands, and specific fevers; on diseases of the blood, for example, anemia; on anomalies of the urinary secretion, for example, lithemia; on local diseases, for example, of the pelvic region and of the rhinopharynx. In what manner these various ailments and conditions cause iridocyclitis, or, to use the more comprehensive term, uveitis, has not been carefully determined. But it does not seem to be unreasonable to assume that it represents an effort on the part of the uveal tract to expel from its tissues some toxin, bacterial or otherwise, precisely as we know that certain forms of dermatitis originate in an effort of the skin to eliminate a poisonous agent. Such an explanation is not a new one. Sydney Stephenson has maintained that inasmuch as many inflammatory affections of the iris and ciliary body are due to microbic infection, there exist good grounds for believing the proximate cause of all cases of endogenous iridocyclitis to be the excretion by the ciliary body of micro-organisms or their products. This excretory effort need not be limited to the ciliary body, but may include the choroid. A significant fact in this connection is the well-known favorable action of pilocarpin in affections of the ciliary body and choroid. Their excretory efforts are increased under the influence of this drug, and hence its curative power. We may say that the uveal tract sweats exactly as does the skin. Time does not permit me to elaborate these suggestions further, or to go more deeply into the etiology of uveitis. I wish now to present for consideration certain clinical types of this affection with illustrative cases.

1. RECURRING AND MALIGNANT UVEITIS TERMINATING IN SECONDARY GLAUCOMA AND CATARACT.

The following cases illustrate this type of the affection and indicate that although the termination in each may be similar, the earliest stages, and in some respects the course of the disease, are not identical.

CASE 1.—A. H. R., aged 35, male, born in Pennsylvania, married, lawyer, consulted me Jan. 16, 1899.

History.—With the exception of the ordinary illnesses of childhood, the patient has always been healthy. He denies venereal disease of any kind and his habits have always been good. His father is alive and a well-preserved man, having no trouble except cataracts. His mother and one aunt died of phthisis. The patient had attacks of inflammation in his right eye when he was a child and has had enlarged lymph glands. Indeed, it is probable that both eyes suffered from attacks of choroiditis in childhood. About ten years before the date of his visit to my office, he consulted an oculist who writes as follows: "The patient came to me about ten years ago with an attack of choroiditis and vitreous opacities of the right eye. The choroid showed the marks of previous attacks in both eyes. Since that time he has had numerous attacks of fresh choroiditis," but apparently no serious involvement of the iris was present in these attacks, at least none is described. The iris became involved three months prior to this examination, i.e., in November, 1898.

Examination.—The patient is a hearty, healthy-looking man, giving no evidence of any constitutional disease.

Eyes.—V. of R. E., fingers at 50 cm. There was marked iridocyclitis with much thickening of the iris, the pupil being semi-dilated, and intense punctate keratitis. A dim red reflex could be obtained from the fundus when the eye was turned up and in, and large black masses could be detected in the vitreous. When the eye was turned down and out, a large elevation was evident of a purplish or of a somewhat violaceous tint, that is to say, a scleral staphyloma. T. was +1. The field was contracted in the manner shown in the diagram (Fig. 1).

V. of L. E. 6/50. The media were clear, the disc of fairly good color; no serious change in the retinal circulation. The entire macular area was occupied by a large expanse of atrophic retino-choroiditis, with patches of atrophy, pigment-

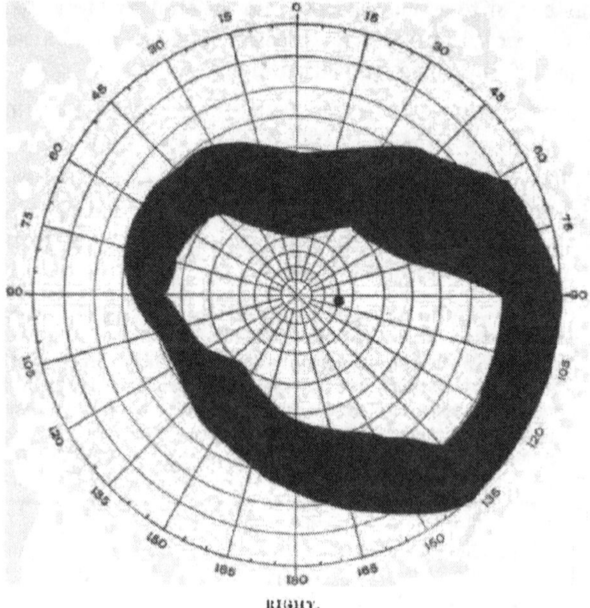

Fig. 1.—Case 1. Visual field, right eye. Malignant uveitis in stage of secondary glaucoma.

heaping and yellow exudate. Under the usual treatment of sweats, mercury, iodids, galvanism and massage, the right eye gradually quieted, that is to say, the marked irido-cyclitis disappeared, but the lens became entirely cataractous and the punctate keratitis changed to a dense infiltration in the lower portion of the cornea. The left eye has continued unchanged and has never shown any signs of punctate keratitis.

Case 2.—C. L. S., aged 23, female, single, born in Pennsylvania, consulted me first May 20, 1895.

History.—When a child the patient‛ in rapid succession had measles, scarlet fever and smallpox. For a year afterwards her eyes were subject to inflammation. At 12 she had malaria and at 16 an attack of "redness in the face" which looked like erysipelas. She has suffered much from menstrual disturbance. The family history is good, parents and brothers and sisters being healthy. In February, 1894, the patient was the subject of an illness, which was characterized by chills intense headache and general fever lasting about a week. I‛ s probable that this was some form of influenza. Soon after

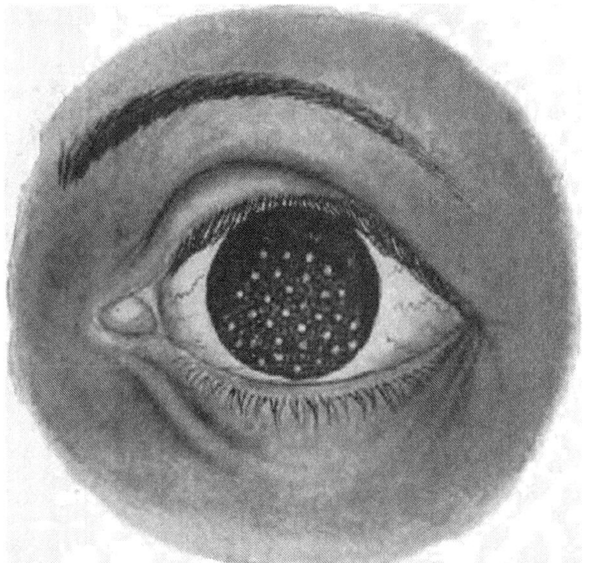

Fig. 2.—Case 2. Malignant uveitis. Early stage. Large dot irregularly placed.

ward the vision of the left eye, which, however, had always been a weak eye since it was ulcerated in early childhood began to fail. Preceding the failure of vision, black spots were much in evidence. Similar failure of vision, but not preceded by any general illness, began in right eye ten months later.

Examination.—The patient is a moderately tall brunette with pallid skin. General examination failed to reveal any lesion of the internal organs. A pelvic examination was no made. The urine was normal and the blood examination wa as follows: Hemoglobin 65 per cent.; red blood corpuscle 4,310,000; leucocytes 10,400. The differential count of th leucocytes was as follows; Neutrophilic polymorphous leucocytes 83.5 per cent.; oxyphilic polymorphous leucocytes 1 per cent.; mononuclear and transitional leucocytes 5 per cent.; lymphocytes 10.3 per cent.

Eyes.—V. of R. E. 6/30; pupil semi-dilated (under the influence of atropin); pigment spots on the capsule of the lens showing the position of former synechiæ. On the posterior surface of the cornea many large dots of gray-white color, somewhat irregularly placed (Fig. 2). The fundus was dimly seen, owing to some opacity in the vitreous. The disc was oval, much congested, and its margins distinctly veiled; the veins were large and tortuous, the arteries about normal in size and the fundus generally edematous.

V. of L. E. fingers at 2 feet; marked punctate keratitis and some striæ in the lens, but cornea and deeper media too hazy to permit any study of the fundus.

Re-examination.—The patient was not seen after this first examination for nearly a year, when she returned with the statement that her eyes had been worse for the past month. Examination now showed unusually large deposits on the posterior surface of each cornea, which could be well studied on the right side (Fig. 3). These dots were gray-white in color and fully a mm. in diameter, the intervening cornea being slightly hazy. Vision was reduced in the right eye to counting fingers at one foot and in the left eye to shadows; no fundus-view on either side.

Treatment.—Under the most vigorous treatment, consisting of sweats, leeching, iodid of potassium, and inunctions of mercury continuing for a year, the vision finally rose in the right eye, with proper correcting glass, to 6/12 and part of 6/9, and in the left eye to 6/60. The spots on the cornea almost disappeared, although a few very fine ones could always be noted in the more dependent portions. During this year there were several attacks which yielded to increased vigor of treatment, one of them being associated with or preceded by a marked gastralgia which lasted for nearly six weeks.

Again the patient was not seen for a year, when she returned with the statement that the vision last recorded had obtained until four weeks prior to her visit, when it began to fail. It was now in the right eye 4/60 and in the left eye 3/100, and the very large spots which had previously been noted were again manifest. For a few months the patient attended irregularly to treatment and then disappeared for a year. At the end of that time, during which she had had numerous attacks, particularly in the spring and summer, associated with severe la grippe, vision was greatly disturbed, being in the right eye about 1/100 and in the left eye fingers at 50 cm. The irides of both eyes were thickened, completely attached to the capsule of the lens and the pupillary spaces occluded with thick membrane. The spots had consolidated, as it were, into an area of thick infiltration at the bottom of each cornea. T. + 1 and the visual fields indicated that secondary glaucomatous conditions were established (Fig. 4).

Operation.—No improvement took place under the ordinary treatment, and on April 19, 1899, iridectomy was performed on the right eye, revealing a partially cataractous lens. Vision improved to the ability to see Sn. 60 at 1 meter. Somewhat later, iridectomy was performed on the left eye, but the coloboma almost immediately closed during an attack which shortly followed the operation. Gradually the cataract thick-

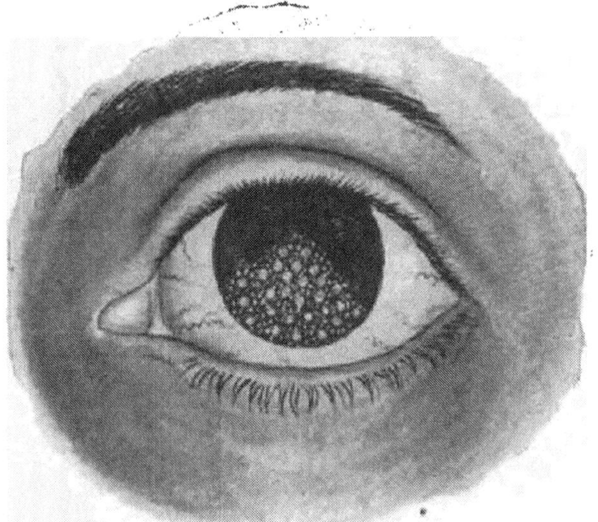

Fig. 3.—Case 3. Early stage of malignant uveitis. Large dots on posterior corneal surface.

ened and became complete about a year after the iridectomy. The patient then drifted into other hands. The cataract was removed, but without materially improving vision. When last examined, in the right eye the coloboma was filled with the remains of cortex and thick lymph, the lower half of the cornea was densely infiltrated; in the left eye, up and out, there was some clear cornea, but elsewhere it was densely infiltrated (Fig. 5).

Case 3.—S. S., aged 20, born in Maryland, single woman, consulted me first April 30, 1898.

History.—There is nothing special in the patient's history, at least in her early history, which throws light on her present condition, and she has not suffered from any severe illness. Both parents are well, two older brothers and sisters and two younger are in good health. One brother, however, has had phthisis. In January, 1898, the right eye became inflamed while the patient was studying at college, which was attributed to hard work and exposure to the bright light from the snow. Gradually the eye got worse, in spite of active and vigorous treatment at the hands of a competent oculist.

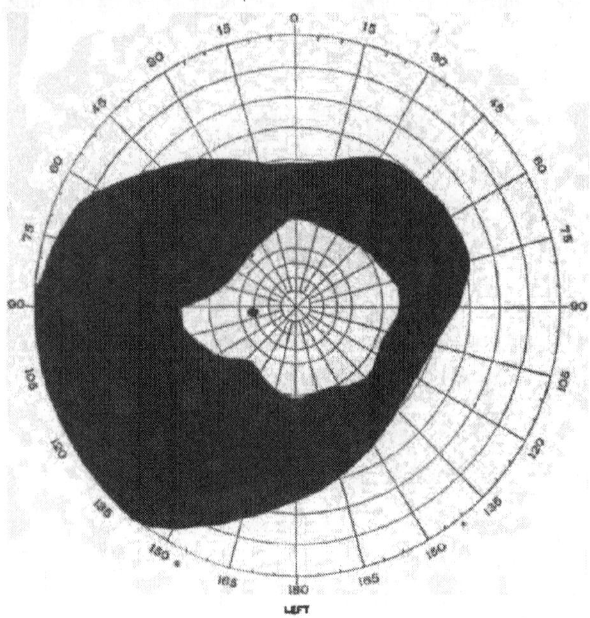

Fig. 4.—Case 2. Visual field, left eye. Malignant uveitis in stage of secondary glaucoma.

Examination.—The patient was a small, slender woman, although with the exception of anemia of the chlorotic type, as evidenced by the blood count, physical examination failed to reveal organic disease. The blood examination was as follows: Color fairly good; coagulation normal; hemoglobin 65 per cent.; red blood corpuscles 4,282,000; leucocytes 11,000; no poikilocytosis. The chest was emphysematous in type, but the respiration was deep and full and the lungs normal in all respects. The cardiac action was rapid and regular and all the sounds clear and distinct, and the cardiac boundaries were normal. The skin of her arms, legs and hands presented an appearance resembling ichthyosis. One brother was similarly affected. The skin is said to be smooth during the summer months.

Eyes.—V. of R. E. fingers at 50 cm.; slight cyclitis; many dots on the posterior layer of the cornea of large size; the lens opaque and swollen; no view of the fundus; only a red reflex. T. + 1. V. of L. E. 6/5, apparently normal in all respects.

The patient was seen from time to time, without material

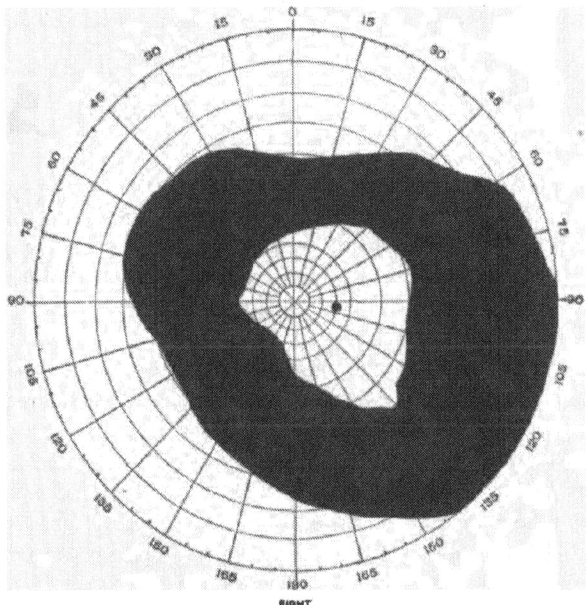

Fig. 4.—Case 2. Visual field, right eye. Malignant uveitis in stage of secondary glaucoma.

alteration in the condition of the right eye, on which operation was not permitted. The cataract gradually became complete and vision was reduced to light perception, the dots on the cornea almost disappearing. In November, 1900, although the vision of the left eye was entirely normal, close examination revealed a faint hyalitis and little areas of edematous haze over the fundus, representing spots of serous infiltration in the choroid. The patient was not seen for six months after this, and then, with slight increase in the vitreous haze and the edematous condition of the choroid, the so-called punctate keratitis was evident, the spots not being very large at this time. The patient stated that three months prior to her visit she had had swelling of the right knee which had disappeared. Examination failed to reveal any lesion in this joint. From this date on to the present time there have been numerous relapses in the left eye with the tendency to form synechiæ, and with each relapse the punctate keratitis has been a little more pronounced and the spots a little greater. The anterior chamber is very deep, but there has been no rise of tension. In addition to the punctate keratitis, the cornea has typically shown the cross-hatched appearance as represented in the diagram (Fig. 6). With the increase in the cross-hatching and punctate condition of the cornea, there has been an increase in the vitreous opacities, which are now dark and floating. The eyeground is difficult to study and shows swollen retinal veins, with fluffy edema of the entire choroid. The visual field is slightly contracted (Fig. 7).

The symptoms and, to a certain extent, the lesions which are common to this class of cases are as follows: Some form of choroiditis; extension of the lesions along the choroidal tract until the ciliary body is involved, followed in turn by participation of the iris in the inflammation; frequent relapses, either of the choroidal disease or of the cyclitic disease, or frequently of both; secondary glaucoma owing to obstruction of the filtrating spaces at the angle of the anterior chamber, dependent in part on the outpouring of cellular elements, in part on a change from the serous to a plastic exudate, and in part on the swelling and pressing forward of the crystalline lens, which, as its nutrition is cut off, becomes cataractous. The corneal lesions in these cases seem to have the following characteristics: An unusual size of the deposits on the posterior lamina, which may or may not have a typical triangular arrangement; a tendency for these deposits to become confluent at the lower portion of the cornea and by pressure to invade the cornea itself in the form of an exudate. The size of these deposits reminds one of those which are often seen in the eyes of colored persons, in which descemetitis is apt to be very pronounced. It has seemed to me that uveitis is apt to be more decided in its mani-

festations in white subjects of the pronounced brun
type.

In one class of these cases of malignant uveitis
primary choroiditis may exist for a long period, dui
which it relapses frequently, prior to the involvemen
the ciliary body and iris; in another class of cases wl
the choroidal lesions are much less marked, they
speedily followed by involvement of the ciliary body
iris and improvement and relapse take place in b
but with each recurrence of the cyclitis improven
becomes more difficult and finally impossible becaus
the disturbance of the nutritive processes in the cil
body and the stoppage of filtration at the angle of

Fig. 5.—Case 2. Malignant uveitis, showing (*b*) large size
coalescence of corneal deposits; (*a*) dense infiltration of the co
at the end stage of the disease.

anterior chamber; finally, in a third class of cases,
process is a continuous one from the start, choroic
rapidly becoming associated with cyclitis, to be follo
quickly by secondary glaucoma and cataract; in ol
words, there are no intermissions. This type of the
ease may be bilateral and quite as severe on one sid
the other, or bilateral, the one eye being blinded
the extension of the inflammatory process, but
other eye saved by a checking of the process in
choroid, or bilateral, the uveitis being malignant fi
the start on one side and similar in character but
malignant on the other side, that is to say, cataract
secondary glaucoma do not appear.

!. ACUTE UVEITIS BEGINNING AS A SCLEROTICO-CHORO-IDITIS, TERMINATING IN MYOPIA AND POS-TERIOR POLAR LENTICULAR OPACITY.

This class will serve to explain, I think, some of the cases of myopia which are encountered, particularly when the myopia is very much more pronounced on one side than on the other, the more myopic eye presenting the remains of the storm in the form of vitreous strings and posterior polar opacity.

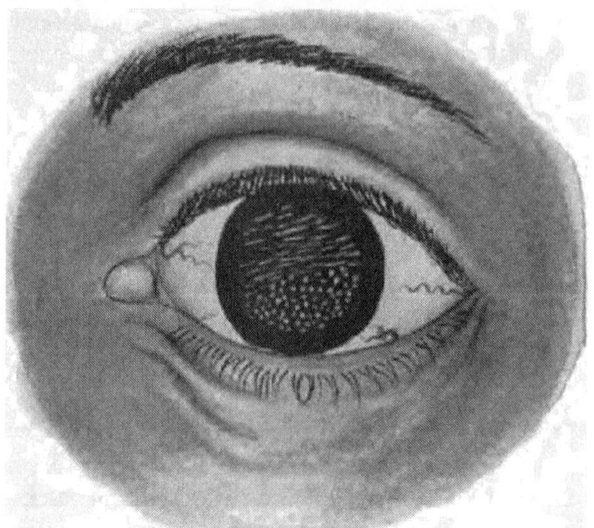

Fig. 6.—Case 3. Uveitis with malignant tendency, showing punc-ate deposits on cornea and cross-hatching.

CASE 4.—J. A. S., aged 22, male, single, born in Pennsylvania, student, consulted me May 2, 1898.

History.—Although never of robust build, the patient has had no serious illness in his life and there is no history of acquired or inherited specific taint. His parents are apparently healthy. During April, 1898, while studying at college, the right eye began to inflame. This inflammation was attributed to hard work and much exposure to artificial light and was unconnected with any illness of a general character.

Examination.—The patient was an under-sized young man

of slender build, with pallid complexion and the general type of features which is described under the term scrofulous. Some acne pimples covered the forehead and face and there was a moderate blepharitis of each eye. Physical examination, however, failed to reveal organic disease in any organ. The urine was normal, there was a moderate amount of swelling of the turbinals, most marked on the right side and some tendency to rhinitis, although this did not appear to be of an infectious character.

Eyes.—V. of R. E. 6/50; typical punctate keratitis and a

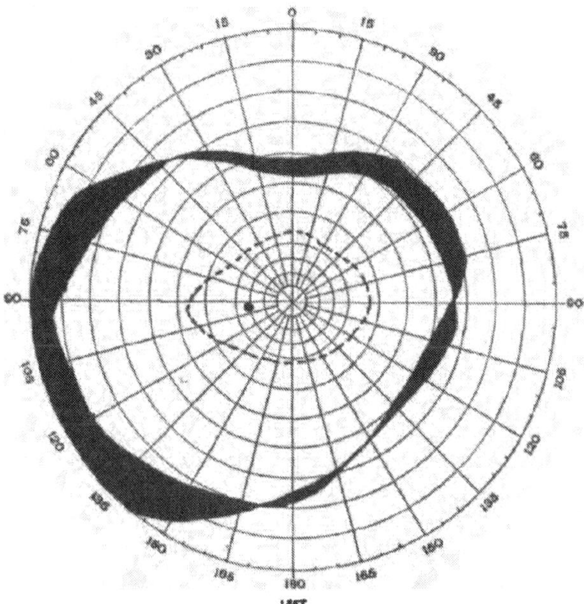

Fig. 7.—Case 3. Visual field, uveitis, with malignant tendency; early stage; slight concentric contraction; general edema of eyeground.

scleral node of violaceous tint, up and out, about the size of a large pea. The corneal spots were of moderate size and rested on a slightly hazy base. The vitreous was full of dark opacities. The disc was a vertical oval, its edges hazy, the veins full and tortuous, and there was a general edematous haze throughout the entire choroid. The field of vision is illustrated in the accompanying diagram (Fig. 8).

2

V. of L. E. was normal, the media clear, and there were no changes in the fundus.

Treatment.—The patient was immediately placed upon treatment consisting of mercurial inunctions, ascending doses of iodid of potassium and pilocarpin sweats, and rapidly improved so that at the end of four months the vision of the right eye was 6/15, the scleral node had disappeared and the iridocyclitis had markedly subsided. Then there was a fresh attack with marked exacerbation of the punctate keratitis and increase in the size of the spots on the posterior layer of the cornea. Gradually, under the influence of pilocarpin sweats, iodid and bichlorid of mercury, the cyclitis subsided, the spots became smaller or disappeared, although the vitreous opacities, which were large and dark, continued. Galvanism was then used and subsequently the patient sent to a warm climate.

Result.—About a year after the last relapse the media were quite clear, with the exception of some large and stringy vitreous opacities and a suggestive haze around the posterior surface of the lens. The eye had now become myopic and under the fullest mydriasis and in the entire absence of iritis, the neutralizing lens was —5⌒—1 axis 105, 6/15. One year later, with comparatively little change in the refractive error, and with only a few strings in the vitreous, there was a well-marked posterior polar opacity in the crystalline lens, the fundus was clear, the disc a vertical oval, no conus, choroid in fairly good condition. The left eye continued to be normal, and its refraction practically emmetropic.

These cases seem to be characterized in general terms by an area of sclerotico-choroiditis, usually placed well forward, and which is evident in the sclera in the form of a staphylomatous bulging; much hyalitis; comparatively slight involvement of the ciliary body and iris and secondary participation of the cornea, upon which the usual deposits appear in moderate degree. Relapses are not uncommon, but under vigorous treatment the eye quiets with the lesions already described, namely, a certain amount of vitreous change and a posterior polar opacity. Doubtless when the area of sclerotico-choroiditis is far forward the involvement of the ciliary body is quickly manifest through an extension of the process, but the entire choroid is also sufficiently affected to permit a distention of the eyeball and a consequent increase of refraction.

3. MILD, CHRONIC, SENILE UVEITIS, ASSOCIATED WITH ANTECEDENT OR SUBSEQUENT HEMORRHAGES IN THE VITREOUS.

That there exists a mild type of uveitis often seen in elderly subjects, characterized by fluffy areas in the choroid, fine hyalitis, a few spots, almost translucent in appearance, on the posterior surface of the cornea, without involvement apparently either of the ciliary body or of the iris, the pupils remaining perfectly

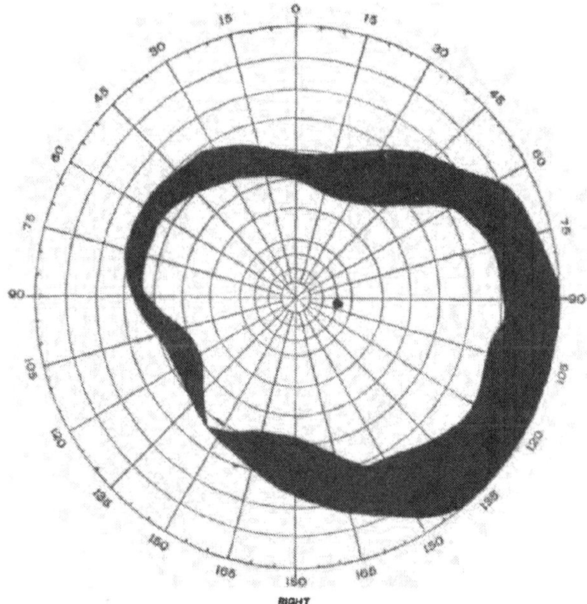

Fig. 8.—Case 4. Visual field, uveitis, beginning as a sclerotico-choroiditis; peripheral contraction; choroiditis also peripheral.

active, is, of course, a very common observation and the symptoms described a familiar picture. The association of retinal hemorrhages, or hemorrhages which burst through the hyaloid into the vitreous is less commonly described and observed.

CASE 5.—Mrs. G. R. B., aged 52, born in America, consulted me first on April 8, 1894.

History.—There is nothing noteworthy in the patient's early history. She had the usual illnesses of childhood, but was in all respects a healthy girl and young woman, except that she suffered from headaches. For the relief of these she was given glasses when twenty years old to correct a high hypermetropic astigmatism. She married young, and has given birth to eight children. Six are living and healthy; two died of scarlet fever. There is no history of influenza. She has occasionally had spells of rheumatism, has suffered sometimes from lumbago, and to use her own expression, "is always taking something for indigestion." She has had much worry

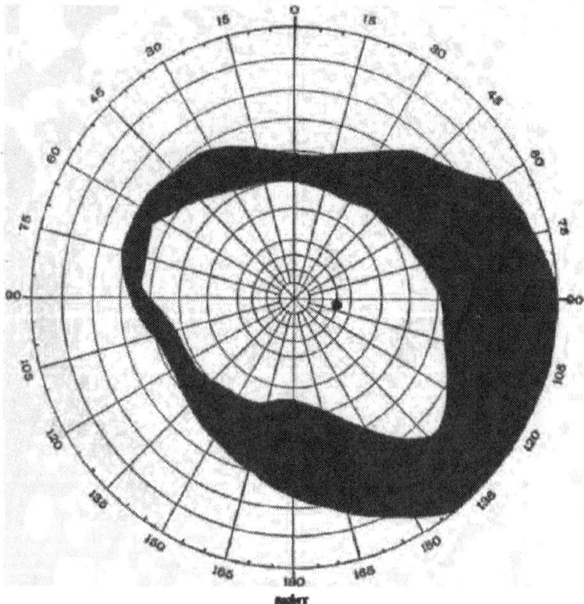

Fig. 9.—Case 6. Visual field, uveitis, following retinal hemorrhage; peripheral contraction; test-object two candles.

during her life, largely owing to her husband's inability to cope with his responsibilities and from the fact that he suffered from epilepsy, his attacks, according to his physician, having been brought into control by the use of mercury. Other than this, however, there is no possible hint of specific infection in this patient.

Examination.—The patient is a well-preserved woman, of good figure and physique, and general examination has failed to reveal any organic disease save only the indigestion before referred to and the tendency to attacks of rheumatism, the word rheumatism being used in the vague sense so constantly given to it. The urine examination was negative; blood examination was not made.

Eyes.—V. of R. E. with correcting glass 6/9. Numerous rather fine translucent dots were present on the posterior sur·face of the cornea, with fine vitreous spots; the disc margins were slightly hazy; the veins were full; the irides prompt in their reaction to light; the anterior chamber deep; and the tension normal.

V. of L. E. with correcting glass 6/9, and an almost exactly similar condition in the cornea and fundus. Somewhat more careful examination a day or two later, after dilatation of the pupil, revealed faint cortical opacities in the periphery of each lens, and between the disc and the macula slight choroidal changes in the form of streaks of erosion. Until the end of the year 1901, or in other words, seven years, the patient was under constant observation, with practically little or no change in the conditions noted. Occasionally the spots on the posterior layer of the cornea would be a little more marked than at other times and the vitreous opacities a little more pronounced. They never entirely cleared away, but also never produced any very serious alteration of vision. Indeed, with full correcting lenses the vision in the right eye was normal and in the left eye 2/3 of normal. Ciliary injection, synechiæ, and inflammatory signs in the iris have never been present.

On the first of January of the present year, after a particularly prolonged season of nursing her sick husband and after reading an unusual amount, dull vision suddenly appeared in the right eye. On examination the vitreous was found entirely filled with large blood-clots.

Treatment and Results.—Under treatment (iodids, mercurials, sweats, etc.), the vitreous entirely cleared, and on the 14th of the past month her vision was 6/9 in that eye and in the opposite eye it was about 6/15. At no time was there any particular change in the visual field, which was normal both peripherally and centrally. After the absorption of the clot, the moderate deposition of dots upon the posterior surface of the cornea was about the same as it had been prior to the hemorrhage, and the only change noted was the very full, dark, somewhat tortuous veins, with signs that they were being pressed on by the arteries.

CASE 6.—M. H., aged 48, female, single, born in Pennsylvania, consulted me first Feb. 24, 1902.

History.—There is nothing of consequence in the patient's history except that she is very rheumatic, or perhaps, more accurately, lithemic. This condition also obtains in members of her family. One brother has had numerous attacks of epi·

scleral congestion of undoubted gouty origin, and is deaf,
probably due to gouty changes in the ear. The patient herself,
however, has been in fairly good condition, and except for a
high astigmatism, has had fairly good eyes. Through her life,
and especially recently, she has had much sorrow and has been
greatly worried and mentally depressed. In October, 1901,
she began, while reading at sea, to have spots and flashes before her eyes, followed a short time afterward by loss of vision.
When examined she was told that she had had a hemorrhage
burst into the vitreous.

Examination.—The patient is a well-formed woman, who

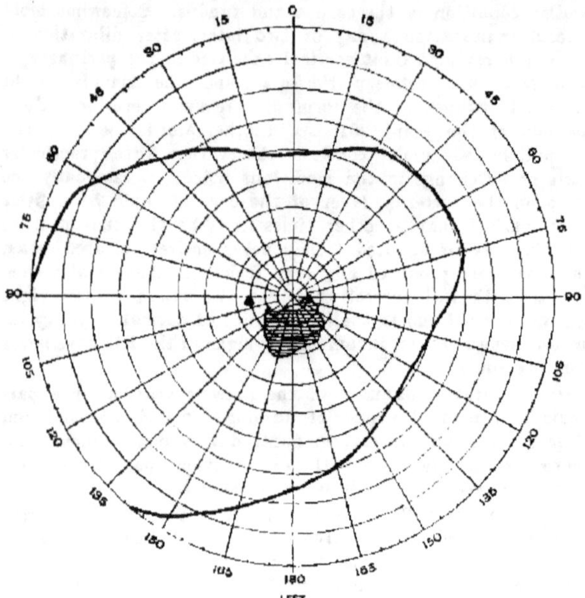

Fig. 10.—Case 7. Visual field, uveitis of gouty origin; negative
scotoma in center of field.

gives no external evidence of disease. Examination of the
heart and lungs failed to reveal any signs of disease. The
blood examination was as follows: Blood fairly good color;
coagulation normal; hemoglobin 66 per cent.; red blood corpuscles 3,920,000; leucocytes 7200; no poikilocytosis. The
urine examination was as follows: Specific gravity 1018; no
albumin; no sugar; urea 1.88 gram per 100 cm.; no casts;
no renal epithelium; a few cylindroids.

Eyes.—V. of R. E. fingers doubtfully in the outer field; no
fundus view, the entire vitreous being obscured with large

dark masses, through the rifts of which a very faint red glare could be obtained. The pupil was normal, the anterior chamber normal; no rise of tension. Field according to the diagram (Fig. 9).

V. of L. E., after the correction of a simple hypermetropic astigmatism, 6/6(?); media clear; round disc of fairly good color; physiologic cup; no fundus lesions.

Treatment and Results.—The only indication for treatment apparently was the simple anemia which the blood count showed, and to which the hemorrhage was ascribed. Remedies,

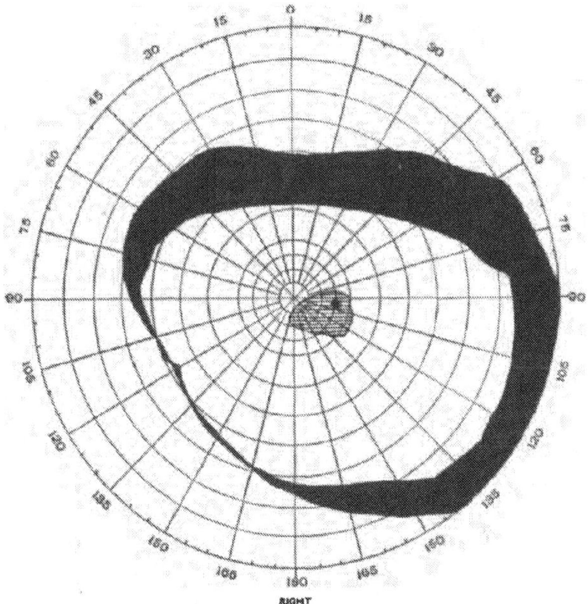

Fig. 10.—Case 7. Visual field, uveitis of gouty origin; negative scotoma in center of field.

however, failed to make any impression, but on April 4 the patient appeared stating that she had had a little pain in the eye. Mild ciliary congestion was evident, with three or four delicate synechiæ and a typical deposition of fine dots upon the posterior layer of the cornea resting upon a hazy surface. The synechiæ readily yielded to the influence of atropin, but the blood clot in the vitreous was unchanged at the last examination.

It would seem that there are two classes of these

cases. In one a mild uveitis, the lesions of which are confined almost entirely, or perhaps entirely, to the choroid, exist for years, iris and ciliary body remaining uninvolved although hyalitis is pronounced. Suddenly hemorrhage bursts into the vitreous, coming either from the ciliary or from the choroidal vessels, it is practically impossible to determine which. The effused blood absorbs perfectly under the ordinary regimen and leaves the eye in practically the same condition that it was before the hemorrhage. In another class it would seem that the ordinary hemorrhages which burst into the vitreous precede by a considerable period of time, it may be months, the appearance of the uveitis. Under these circumstances the hemorrhage in the vitreous is much more pronounced, that is to say, it fails to yield to ordinary treatment, and is followed by descemetitis with involvement of the ciliary body and iris. Significant symptoms in the fundus in cases of this character, when the fundus can be studied, are, in the first place, large tortuous veins pressed on by slightly sclerotic arteries, moderate haziness and swelling of the margins of the disc, and particularly fluffy islands of small exudate and edema, often lying far out in the periphery of the eyeground and chiefly situated along the vessels of larger caliber; rarely small capillary hemorrhages in similar situations.

4. RELAPSING PLASTIC UVEITIS BEGINNING INSIDIOUSLY IN GOUTY AND RHEUMATIC SUBJECTS.

The relapsing iritis so commonly ascribed to gout and rheumatism and so frequently encountered, is not exactly the type to which reference is made under the present heading. Certain cases are offered in illustration.

CASE 7.—Mrs. H. C. H., aged 55, born in Pennsylvania, consulted me on November 3, 1897.

History.—There is nothing of interest in the patient's early history. She comes from a sturdy line of ancestors, all of whom, however, have—to speak in general terms—been gouty. Her children are healthy and exhibit no signs of disease. She herself has suffered from vague pains, and after middle life was greatly afflicted with pain in the sole of her foot and the arch of her toe, which was attributed to gout. She has been in the habit of leading a rather lazy life so far as physical exertion is concerned, but has been mentally very active. On November 7, 1897, she began to complain of flitting clouds and specks before the right eye, which soon made their appearance before the left eye also.

Examination.—The patient was too stout and moved with some difficulty, owing partly to her disinclination to make physical exertion and partly to the pain which walking occasioned in her feet. Repeated examinations by the most skilful physicians failed to detect the slightest evidence of disease in her heart, general circulation or kidneys. In general terms, however, these examinations did reveal an excess of uric acid.

Eyes.—V. of R. E., after the correction of a slight hypermetropic astigmatism, normal; the disc was oval, of fairly good color, the veins full and irregular, with a slight tendency to beading. There was a faint grayish haze throughout the retina and some superficial choroidal disturbance (epithelial choroiditis).

V. of L. E. normal and exactly similar ophthalmoscopic conditions; media of both eyes clear; pupil reactions normal. Two months later the muscæ had assumed the appearance of clouds, somewhat orange-colored, and an examination of the field of vision revealed perhaps slight concentric contraction and almost symmetrical color scotomas, situated slightly below and more to the temporal than to the nasal side of the fixation point (Fig. 10).

Subsequent History.—The patient was not seen again until Oct. 21, 1898, when she returned with the history that while abroad and on the 2d of April, that is to say, three months after the last examination, she developed iritis. She was treated in France and England and from her English physician I know that when he first saw her the signs were only those of iritis or iridocyclitis, but later on, that is to say, just prior to her return to this country in October, deposits on Descemet's membrane, the so-called punctate keratitis, were easily visible. Peripheral choroiditis, however, was not at that time demonstrated. When examined again by me the right eye showed well-marked uveitis, punctate spots on the cornea, hyalitis, fogginess and edema of the choroid, and great distention of the retinal circulation. V. = 6/50. In the left eye V. = 6/5; the remains of synechia below; some faint vitreous haze; a few spots on the posterior surface of the cornea.

From that date until June, 1901, this patient has had numerous attacks and relapses, sometimes in one, sometimes in the other eye, and a few times in both eyes. The attacks always begin with clouds followed soon by slight ciliary congestion, the formation of synechiæ if not prevented with atropin, increase in the hyalitis and marked increase in the punctate deposits on the cornea and the cross-hatching in this membrane. Since the last date noted there has been no attack, the good result apparently being largely due to systematic treatment by baths in the Hot Springs. Vision is now normal in each eye, although there are still faint opacities on the posterior surface of each cornea, most marked upon the right side, and a few fine vitreous changes.

CASE 8.—Mrs. J. S., aged 47, born in the United States, consulted me Oct. 17, 1901.

History.—There is nothing in the patient's early history which bears directly upon her subsequent ocular disturbance. Her chief illnesses apparently occurred after she was grown up and after her marriage. She has always been typically rheumatic. Some six or seven years ago she had an attack of rheumatism lasting for a long time and treated with large doses of salicylate of sodium. To this drug the patient attributed much of her deafness, which was very pronounced and which had been associated with middle-ear disease and chronic naso-pharyngeal catarrh. She has had several operations on her nose, probably removal of hypertrophied turbinates. She has also had some abdominal operation the nature of which was not definitely ascertained, probably an ovariotomy. One year ago she suffered much from furunculosis, and in the winter of 1900 from severe influenza. The patient's father is dead; her mother is living and healthy; one sister is living, who is also very rheumatic. The patient's eyesight has always been good; indeed, she has prided herself upon her good eyesight until May, 1901, when she suffered from flitting episcleral congestions. These were attributed by her attending physician to eyestrain, co-incident with beginning presbyopia and glasses were ordered. From time to time these ocular congestions recurred, but were unassociated with severe pain until about three or four months later, when violent pain occurred. The eyes, however, were examined at that time by an expert ophthalmologist, and according to the patient's statements, no very good reason for the pain was discovered. From August, 1901, until the middle of October, 1901, the patient seems to have suffered from frequent attacks of ocular congestion, but did not consult any one for her relief.

Examination.—The patient is a good-sized, very blonde woman, with pallid skin and slightly bluish lips. The heart sounds were feeble, but there were no murmurs or signs of organic disease. Examination of the urine was as follows: Specific gravity 1022; albumin none; sugar none; urea 4.5 grains to the fluid ounce; urates not increased; chlorias normal; phosphates greatly diminished; sulphates slightly in-

creased. In the sediment were found many pus cells and much bladder epithelium and mucous shreds; many cylindroids but no true casts. The patient was quite deaf, being able to distinguish only very loudly-spoken words. There was well-marked atrophic rhinitis.

Eyes.—V. of R. E. 6/15; well-marked punctate keratitis, the spots being somewhat irregularly placed and not of very great size; anterior chamber about normal in depth; thick irregular synechia, firmly attaching the edge of the pupil to the iris. The disc was vertically oval in shape. No special changes could be discovered in the fundus; opacities floated in the vitreous.

V. of L. E. 6/22; similar conditions, with the exception of much more marked synechia and plastic exudate binding down the pupillary area.

Treatment and Results.—From the middle of October until the middle of March, the patient suffered numerous relapses, sometimes in one and sometimes in the other eye, lasting from a few hours to five or six days, and always accompanied by the most excruciating pain. All manner of treatment was tried—inunctions, sweats, the iodids, salicylates, leeching, coal-tar products, etc. All of them were unavailing except the salicylates, or some anti-rheumatic remedy. These always controlled the attacks. On a few occasions, when they were very severe, recourse was had to morphia. Always during the attack there was marked increase in the bulbar injection, great increase in the corneal haziness and deposition of the corneal dots, with such great tenderness in the ciliary region that it was difficult to ascertain anything by palpation. Gradually the violence of the attacks subsided, and by the middle of March, although the synechiæ, previously described, which had been so plastic in type that they had been utterly uninfluenced by the mydriatics, remained, the eyes were white and quiet and vision, with suitable correction, was 6/9 in each. The patient was then sent to the Hot Springs for a cure, where she remained for two months. Since then there have been fewer recurrences of the attacks, but the pupillary spaces are so much blocked with lymph that iridectomies are urgently required.

The approach of this type of the disease, which I have ventured to denominate insidious, is from two regions. In one class of cases the primary lesion appears in the fundus in the form of an ill-defined choroidal change, or patches of ill-defined choroiditis, while the visual field, but little contracted in its periphery, presents in various portions of its center ill-defined scotomas, and the patient is seriously annoyed by obscurations in the visual field and various types of muscæ, although vitreous change can not be found at this time and direct vision may be normal. Later, it may be months afterwards, the first signs of iritis appear, or more accurately, iridocyclitis, followed sooner or later by the punctate deposits on the cornea, the vitreous changes, etc., the exudate in the pupil space assuming a distinctly plastic nature, so that unless atropin is promptly and speedily used the iris is bound down to the lens capsule by firm synechiæ. Case 7 illustrates this type of the disease very well. In the second class the first symptoms which ought to call attention to the disease appear in the form of flitting conjunctival episcleral congestions, the "hot eye" of Jonathan Hutchinson, the "vasomotor dilatation of the vessels" of Swan M. Burnett, and the "fugacious periodic episcleritis" of Fuchs. That singularly acute observer, Jonathan Hutchinson, long ago stated that this conjunctival, or conjunctivo-scleral condition, might be antecedent to an inflammation of the iris and ciliary body, which, when it comes, may assume the typical relapsing character, associated with corneal lesions and dense vitreous exudates and thick plastic material in the pupil space, which is described in Case 8. Had this patient's condition been recognized when she first applied for treatment, as is described in her case history, months, certainly weeks, before the iritis appeared, her subsequent serious suffering might have been avoided.

ANALYSIS OF THIRTY-SEVEN CASES OF UVEITIS.

HIRAM WOODS.
BALTIMORE.

The form of uveitis I propose to consider is choroido-cyclitis. The cases, with two exceptions, were seen in private practice. They divide themselves naturally into those with and without descemetitis. This was found in twenty of my thirty-seven cases: two of serous iritis and eighteen of choroiditis with descemititis. The closest description I have found in text-books of this form of choroiditis is by A. Hill Griffith in Norris' and Oliver's "System." Under the heading "Anomalous Forms" he describes a "Choroiditis with Descemetitis." He had seen forty or fifty cases, chiefly in young women. His explanation of the descemetitis is: "The dots on Descemet's membrane are formed in the choroid, set free in the vitreous and carried by the nutrient currents of the eye to be deposited on the back of the cornea, which view necessitates the permeability of the suspensory ligament by solid particles."

As to causation, syphilis was never found. Anemia and tuberculous family history were sometimes present, and the cases treated accordingly; but in many the cause was undetermined. My own cases confirm this difficulty of fixing a cause. In giving as "causes" associated life epoch or functional defect, I mean only to suggest such inference as can be drawn from association in a number of cases. As descemetitis is the boundary between this and other forms of choroiditis observed, it

History.—There is nothing noteworthy in the patient's early history. She had the usual illnesses of childhood, but was in all respects a healthy girl and young woman, except that she suffered from headaches. For the relief of these she was given glasses when twenty years old to correct a high hypermetropic astigmatism. She married young, and has given birth to eight children. Six are living and healthy; two died of scarlet fever. There is no history of influenza. She has occasionally had spells of rheumatism, has suffered sometimes from lumbago, and to use her own expression, "is always taking something for indigestion." She has had much worry

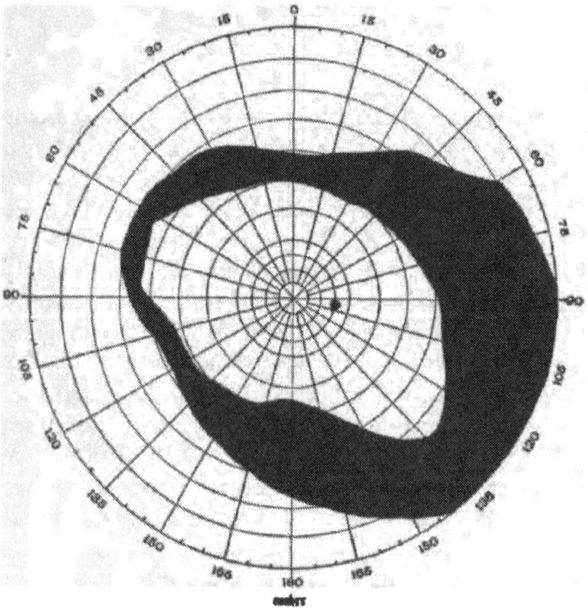

Fig. 9.—Case 6. Visual field, uveitis, following retinal hemorrhage; peripheral contraction; test-object two candles.

during her life, largely owing to her husband's inability to cope with his responsibilities and from the fact that he suffered from epilepsy, his attacks, according to his physician, having been brought into control by the use of mercury. Other than this, however, there is no possible hint of specific infection in this patient.

Examination.—The patient is a well-preserved woman, of good figure and physique, and general examination has failed to reveal any organic disease save only the indigestion before referred to and the tendency to attacks of rheumatism, the word rheumatism being used in the vague sense so constantly given to it. The urine examination was negative; blood examination was not made.

Eyes.—V. of R. E. with correcting glass 6/9. Numerous rather fine translucent dots were present on the posterior surface of the cornea, with fine vitreous spots; the disc margins were slightly hazy; the veins were full; the irides prompt in their reaction to light; the anterior chamber deep; and the tension normal.

V. of L. E. with correcting glass 6/9, and an almost exactly similar condition in the cornea and fundus. Somewhat more careful examination a day or two later, after dilatation of the pupil, revealed faint cortical opacities in the periphery of each lens, and between the disc and the macula slight choroidal changes in the form of streaks of erosion. Until the end of the year 1901, or in other words, seven years, the patient was under constant observation, with practically little or no change in the conditions noted. Occasionally the spots on the posterior layer of the cornea would be a little more marked than at other times and the vitreous opacities a little more pronounced. They never entirely cleared away, but also never produced any very serious alteration of vision. Indeed, with full correcting lenses the vision in the right eye was normal and in the left eye 2/3 of normal. Ciliary injection, synechiæ, and inflammatory signs in the iris have never been present.

On the first of January of the present year, after a particularly prolonged season of nursing her sick husband and after reading an unusual amount, dull vision suddenly appeared in the right eye. On examination the vitreous was found entirely filled with large blood-clots.

Treatment and Results.—Under treatment (iodids, mercurials, sweats, etc.), the vitreous entirely cleared, and on the 14th of the past month her vision was 6/9 in that eye and in the opposite eye it was about 6/15. At no time was there any particular change in the visual field, which was normal both peripherally and centrally. After the absorption of the clot, the moderate deposition of dots upon the posterior surface of the cornea was about the same as it had been prior to the hemorrhage, and the only change noted was the very full, dark, somewhat tortuous veins, with signs that they were being pressed on by the arteries.

Case 6.—M. H., aged 48, female, single, born in Pennsylvania, consulted me first Feb. 24, 1902.

History.—There is nothing of consequence in the patient's history except that she is very rheumatic, or perhaps, more accurately, lithemic. This condition also obtains in members of her family. One brother has had numerous attacks of episcleral congestion of undoubted gouty origin, and is deaf, probably due to gouty changes in the ear. The patient herself, however, has been in fairly good condition, and except for a high astigmatism, has had fairly good eyes. Through her life, and especially recently, she has had much sorrow and has been greatly worried and mentally depressed. In October, 1901, she began, while reading at sea, to have spots and flashes before her eyes, followed a short time afterward by loss of vision. When examined she was told that she had had a hemorrhage burst into the vitreous.

Examination.—The patient is a well-formed woman, who

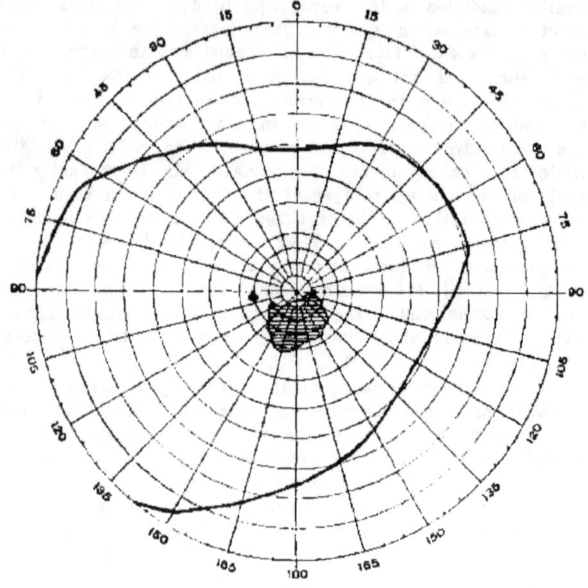

Fig. 10.—Case 7. Visual field, uveitis of gouty origin; negative scotoma in center of field.

gives no external evidence of disease. Examination of the heart and lungs failed to reveal any signs of disease. The blood examination was as follows: Blood fairly good color; coagulation normal; hemoglobin 66 per cent.; red blood corpuscles 3,920,000; leucocytes 7200; no poikilocytosis. The urine examination was as follows: Specific gravity 1018; no albumin; no sugar; urea 1.88 gram per 100 cm.; no casts; no renal epithelium; a few cylindroids.

Eyes.—V. of R. E. fingers doubtfully in the outer field; no fundus view, the entire vitreous being obscured with large

of serous iritis, there are thirteen cases in the female sex, in nine of whom uveitis made its first appearance during the early years of menstrual life, this function being, so far as known, normal in four, abnormal in five. Three of the four relapsing cases were under the care of gynecologists. It is impossible to say whether the pelvic trouble causes the eye lesion or if both are due to some hemic or other influence at present unknown.

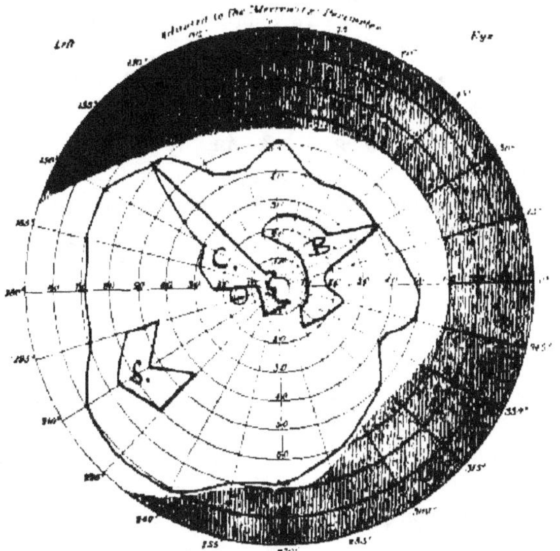

Fig. 2.—B and C. Areas of color scotoma and dim white perception. S. Absolute transient scotoma. Field limits narrowed.

To summarize: This form of choroiditis seems to differ from others, 1, in ophthalmoscopic appearances; 2, mode of onset and early symptoms; 3, etiology, so far as we are aware; 4, prognosis. Some of them get entirely well by absorption of exudate, but, especially if atrophy remains, there is great danger of relapse. This may continue indefinitely, but so long as the fovea is spared, useful vision remains. A woman of 42 gave history of six attacks, during each of which she was prac-

cases. In one a mild uveitis, the lesions of which are confined almost entirely, or perhaps entirely, to the choroid, exist for years, iris and ciliary body remaining uninvolved although hyalitis is pronounced. Suddenly hemorrhage bursts into the vitreous, coming either from the ciliary or from the choroidal vessels, it is practically impossible to determine which. The effused blood absorbs perfectly under the ordinary regimen and leaves the eye in practically the same condition that it was before the hemorrhage. In another class it would seem that the ordinary hemorrhages which burst into the vitreous precede by a considerable period of time, it may be months, the appearance of the uveitis. Under these circumstances the hemorrhage in the vitreous is much more pronounced, that is to say, it fails to yield to ordinary treatment, and is followed by descemetitis with involvement of the ciliary body and iris. Significant symptoms in the fundus in cases of this character, when the fundus can be studied, are, in the first place, large tortuous veins pressed on by slightly sclerotic arteries, moderate haziness and swelling of the margins of the disc, and particularly fluffy islands of small exudate and edema, often lying far out in the periphery of the eyeground and chiefly situated along the vessels of larger caliber; rarely small capillary hemorrhages in similar situations.

4. RELAPSING PLASTIC UVEITIS BEGINNING INSIDIOUSLY IN GOUTY AND RHEUMATIC SUBJECTS.

The relapsing iritis so commonly ascribed to gout and rheumatism and so frequently encountered, is not exactly the type to which reference is made under the present heading. Certain cases are offered in illustration.

CASE 7.—Mrs. H. C. H., aged 55, born in Pennsylvania, consulted me on November 3, 1897.

History.—There is nothing of interest in the patient's early history. She comes from a sturdy line of ancestors, all of whom, however, have—to speak in general terms—been gouty. Her children are healthy and exhibit no signs of disease. She herself has suffered from vague pains, and after middle life was greatly afflicted with pain in the sole of her foot and the arch of her toe, which was attributed to gout. She has been in the habit of leading a rather lazy life so far as physical exertion is concerned, but has been mentally very active. On November 7, 1897, she began to complain of flitting clouds and specks before the right eye, which soon made their appearance before the left eye also.

Examination.—The patient was too stout and moved with some difficulty, owing partly to her disinclination to make physical exertion and partly to the pain which walking occasioned in her feet. Repeated examinations by the most skilful physicians failed to detect the slightest evidence of disease in her heart, general circulation or kidneys. In general terms, however, these examinations did reveal an excess of uric acid.

Eyes.—V. of R. E., after the correction of a slight hypermetropic astigmatism, normal; the disc was oval, of fairly good color, the veins full and irregular, with a slight tendency to beading. There was a faint grayish haze throughout the retina and some superficial choroidal disturbance (epithelial choroiditis).

V. of L. E. normal and exactly similar ophthalmoscopic conditions; media of both eyes clear; pupil reactions normal. Two months later the muscæ had assumed the appearance of clouds, somewhat orange-colored, and an examination of the field of vision revealed perhaps slight concentric contraction and almost symmetrical color scotomas, situated slightly below and more to the temporal than to the nasal side of the fixation point (Fig. 10).

Subsequent History.—The patient was not seen again until Oct. 21, 1898, when she returned with the history that while abroad and on the 2d of April, that is to say, three months after the last examination, she developed iritis. She was treated in France and England and from her English physician I know that when he first saw her the signs were only those of iritis or iridocyclitis, but later on, that is to say, just prior to her return to this country in October, deposits on Descemet's membrane, the so-called punctate keratitis, were easily visible. Peripheral choroiditis, however, was not at that time demonstrated. When examined again by me the right eye showed well-marked uveitis, punctate spots on the cornea, hyalitis, fogginess and edema of the choroid, and great distention of the retinal circulation. V. = 6/50. In the left eye V. = 6/5; the remains of synechia below; some faint vitreous haze; a few spots on the posterior surface of the cornea.

From that date until June, 1901, this patient has had numerous attacks and relapses, sometimes in one, sometimes in the other eye, and a few times in both eyes. The attacks always begin with clouds followed soon by slight ciliary congestion, the formation of synechiæ if not prevented with atropin, increase in the hyalitis and marked increase in the punctate deposits on the cornea and the cross-hatching in this membrane. Since the last date noted there has been no attack, the good result apparently being largely due to systematic treatment by baths in the Hot Springs. Vision is now normal in each eye, although there are still faint opacities on the posterior surface of each cornea, most marked upon the right side, and a few fine vitreous changes.

CASE 8.—Mrs. J. S., aged 47, born in the United States, consulted me Oct. 17, 1901.

History.—There is nothing in the patient's early history which bears directly upon her subsequent ocular disturbance. Her chief illnesses apparently occurred after she was grown up and after her marriage. She has always been typically rheumatic. Some six or seven years ago she had an attack of rheumatism lasting for a long time and treated with large doses of salicylate of sodium. To this drug the patient attributed much of her deafness, which was very pronounced and which had been associated with middle-ear disease and chronic naso-pharyngeal catarrh. She has had several operations on her nose, probably removal of hypertrophied turbinates. She has also had some abdominal operation the nature of which was not definitely ascertained, probably an ovariotomy. One year ago she suffered much from furunculosis, and in the winter of 1900 from severe influenza. The patient's father is dead; her mother is living and healthy; one sister is living, who is also very rheumatic. The patient's eyesight has always been good; indeed, she has prided herself upon her good eyesight until May, 1901, when she suffered from flitting episcleral congestions. These were attributed by her attending physician to eyestrain, co-incident with beginning presbyopia and glasses were ordered. From time to time these ocular congestions recurred, but were unassociated with severe pain until about three or four months later, when violent pain occurred. The eyes, however, were examined at that time by an expert ophthalmologist, and according to the patient's statements, no very good reason for the pain was discovered. From August, 1901, until the middle of October, 1901, the patient seems to have suffered from frequent attacks of ocular congestion, but did not consult any one for her relief.

Examination.—The patient is a good-sized, very blonde woman, with pallid skin and slightly bluish lips. The heart sounds were feeble, but there were no murmurs or signs of organic disease. Examination of the urine was as follows: Specific gravity 1022; albumin none; sugar none; urea 4.5 grains to the fluid ounce; urates not increased; chlorids normal; phosphates greatly diminished; sulphates slightly increased. In the sediment were found many pus cells and much bladder epithelium and mucous shreds; many cylindroids but no true casts. The patient was quite deaf, being able to distinguish only very loudly-spoken words. There was well-marked atrophic rhinitis.

Eyes.—V. of R. E. 6/15; well-marked punctate keratitis, the spots being somewhat irregularly placed and not of very great size; anterior chamber about normal in depth; thick irregular synechia, firmly attaching the edge of the pupil to the iris. The disc was vertically oval in shape. No special changes could be discovered in the fundus; opacities floated in the vitreous.

V. of L. E. 6/22; similar conditions, with the exception of much more marked synechia and plastic exudate binding down the pupillary area.

Treatment and Results.—From the middle of October until the middle of March, the patient suffered numerous relapses, sometimes in one and sometimes in the other eye, lasting from a few hours to five or six days, and always accompanied by the most excruciating pain. All manner of treatment was tried—inunctions, sweats, the iodids, salicylates, leeching, coal-tar products, etc. All of them were unavailing except the salicylates, or some anti-rheumatic remedy. These always controlled the attacks. On a few occasions, when they were very severe, recourse was had to morphia. Always during the attack there was marked increase in the bulbar injection, great increase in the corneal haziness and deposition of the corneal dots, with such great tenderness in the ciliary region that it was difficult to ascertain anything by palpation. Gradually the violence of the attacks subsided, and by the middle of March, although the synechiæ, previously described, which had been so plastic in type that they had been utterly uninfluenced by the mydriatics, remained, the eyes were white and quiet and vision, with suitable correction, was 6/9 in each. The patient was then sent to the Hot Springs for a cure, where she remained for two months. Since then there have been fewer recurrences of the attacks, but the pupillary spaces are so much blocked with lymph that iridectomies are urgently required.

The approach of this type of the disease, which I have ventured to denominate insidious, is from two regions. In one class of cases the primary lesion appears in the fundus in the form of an ill-defined choroidal change, or patches of ill-defined choroiditis, while the visual field, but little contracted in its periphery, presents in various portions of its center ill-defined scotomas, and the patient is seriously annoyed by ob-

kept the eye sensitive and finally produced ophthalmo-scopic choroido-retinitis.

In the following three cases changes followed each other in such rapid succession as to leave no doubt that the red disc and vitreous opacities meant serious trouble. A lady, 31 years of age, was seen in December, 1900, for defective central vision in the left eye. She had consulted another oculist a month previous, who had found choroiditis, and given an unfavorable prog-

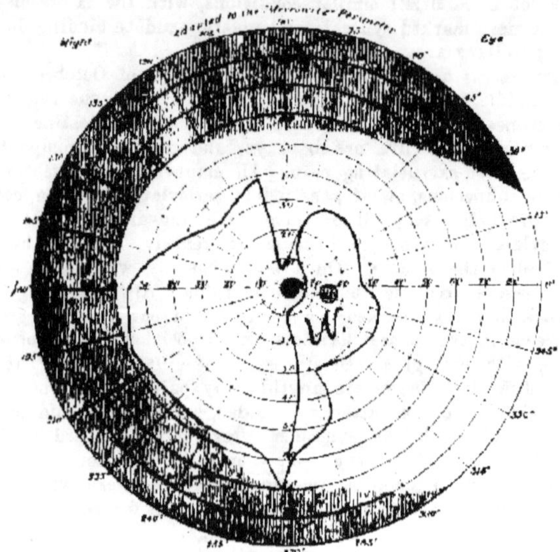

Figure 7.

Figs. 5, 6, 7 show progressive narrowing of right temporal field; letters Y, X, W, color scotomata and dim white areas always preceding loss of portion of field.

nosis. Vision was 20/70, with a paracentral scotoma (Fig. 1). Red disc, floating vitreous opacities and perifoveal pigment heaps were present. In eighteen months fundal appearances have not materially changed. In March, 1902, she thought this eye was getting worse. Examination showed a peripheral positive scotoma and two field areas in which colors were lost and white was

dim (Fig. 2). On May 27 the shape of the dim areas had
changed, and scotoma disappeared (Fig. 3). In the right
eye, which was examined and found normal in December,
1900, visual changes have progressed. In February,
1901, she complained of pain, which yielded to atropia.
Vision was 20/15, field normal, but accommodation had
fallen off. She needed +2 D. to read 1 Jaeg. I found
a few small muscæ in the anterior vitreous, and reddened disc. A month later a small choroido-retinal

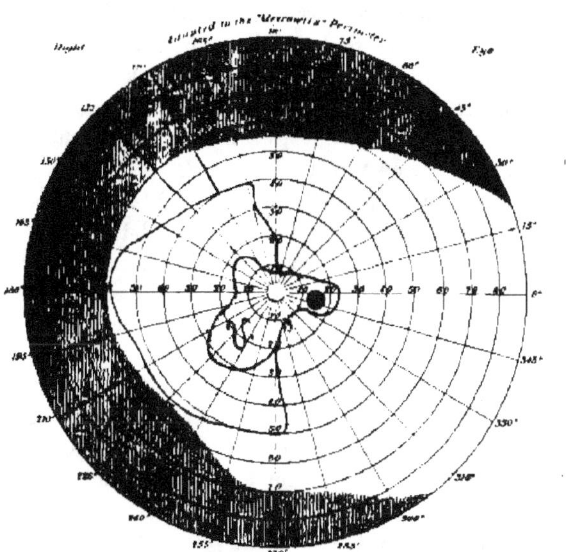

Fig. 8.—Only a little temporal field left. Nasal field contracting.
Space V, color scotoma, as in other figures, encroaching well into
nasal field.

exudate was found in lower nasal fundus, only after
careful search, and field examination had demonstrated
narrowing up and out·(Fig. 4). From this there have
developed in the temporal field dim areas as described
above, soon becoming scotomatous and gradually ap-
proaching the fovea (Figs. 5, 6 and 7). Central vision
was affected only after nine months, when it was 20/30,
with complete loss of temporal field. The dim area has

now crossed into the nasal field, and central vision is reduced to 20/70 (Fig. 8). Only hyperemic discs, floating bodies in a clear vitreous and insignificant peripheral changes have been found. It seems to me that atrophy of the retinal cells is the only explanation dependent upon a pre-existing choroiditis, possibly, or an independent retinal affection from the same cause which produced the signs of choroidal hyperemia, as held by Griffith. In this case no cause was found, unless it was an offensive post-nasal catarrh. It is possibly worthy of remark that the father of this lady once had what was called "hyalitis," from which he recovered. He himself, a very intelligent man, while understanding the causes of such things, could throw no light on the etiology in his own or his daughter's case.

The two other patients were men, 37 and 40, both in robust health, free, so far as could be determined, from syphilis or tuberculosis, one a farmer, the other a country merchant. Both consulted me for the same symptoms—asthenopia in reading and muscæ. Both eyes were involved in one, the muscaæ being seen only by the left eye in the other. Central and peripheral vision was normal in the first case in both eyes. The discs were red, vitreous, cloudy and contained many opacities, but no fundal exudate or hemorrhage was found. In a few months both eyes had detached retina and secondary cataracts formed later. Removal of these has given ability to walk alone. The other man of 40 presented similar red discs with vitreous opacities. The left eye presented a small peripheral retinal extravasation. Central vision was 20/20 R., 20/70 L. E. The right eye has developed only defective accommodation found at first. With emmetropic refraction he needs at 40 +1. for near. The left eye is lost, save in lower periphery of field, by detached retina and vitreous clouds. Here, then, are six cases, all free from syphilis, tuberculosis, central lesion or suspicion of toxic disturbance. All showed the same initial fundal lesion, red disc, the accepted sign of choroidal hyperemia and vitreous opacities. In three there was abnormally low accommodation. One had no lessening of visual acuity, one a scotoma which disappears with rest, a third developed, after years, an exudate. Three patients lost useful sight by retinal atrophy or retinal detachment.

To conclude, the 37 cases indicate: 1. That ·menstruation, in its establishment, or later, if abnormal, intestinal disorders, acute infections and nasopharyngeal disease should be reckoned among possible causes of plastic choroiditis. Whether or not these conditions are themselves direct causes or lower resisting powers and so enable other causes to act, is uncertain. Nor can it be definitely said that some of these coincident conditions may not themselves be manifestations of recognized causes of uveitis; rheumatism, anemia and the like. 2. These cases of obscure etiology show greater tendency to relapse than forms whose cause is better known. They almost invariably show descemetitis. 3. The fundal changes of so-called "choroidal hyperemia," especially if accompanied by defective accommodation and vitreous opacities, demand guarded prognosis and repeated examination for dim field areas.

842 Park Avenue.

THE DIAGNOSTIC IMPORTANCE OF KERATITIS PUNCTATA INTERNA (DESCEMETITIS).

HARRY FRIEDENWALD, A.B., M.D.
BALTIMORE.

The term keratitis punctata is applied to several very different conditions. We must distinguish between the true punctate inflammations, the keratitis punctata profunda, the keratitis punctata superficialis, etc., and that form which consists of deposits on the inner surface of the cornea. If we retain the term for this form we should define it as "keratitis punctata interna." This condition is also known by the name of descemetitis, and, while there are objections to this term, it is less liable to produce confusion, and for this reason and for the sake of brevity we shall use it in this paper.

In a paper published in the Archives of Ophthalmology[1] six years ago, I brought evidence to show that descemetitis occurs in every case of iritis. I divided the descemetitis into two forms—the coarse, which can be seen with the naked eye, and the fine, which is detected by means of strong convex lenses behind the ophthalmoscope. The former is occasional, the latter constant. It is the coarse variety only to which most writers refer under the term of descemetitis.

Concerning the position which these deposits take, little need be said. The coarser opacities are found chiefly or entirely in the lower half of the cornea, frequently arranged in the well-known triangular form.

---

1. Vol. xxv, 1896, p. 191.

In rare cases the entire inner surface is covered. The fine opacities are also most abundant in the lower half, but frequently cover the upper half as well. Exceptional cases occur in which the spots cover an area more or less central. The largest spots rarely exceed one mm. in diameter and are usually round. In very rare cases they assume irregular forms and become much larger. In a case of tubercular iritis which recently came under my observation, they were so large and so much resembled the miliary tubercles on the surface of the iris that I assumed that they were likewise of a tubercular nature.

In order to learn the facts as to the occurrence of descemetitis in various diseases of the eye, I have carefully reviewed my case—histories both hospital and private for the past twelve years. This paper is a summary of these cases, together with the conclusions to which they lead. Assuming that my statement that descemetitis occurs in every case of iritis is accepted by all who have given this subject any study, I shall refrain from citing in this paper several hundred cases in which this condition depended upon iritis. I may add that observations since the publication of my former paper have corroborated the views then expressed. I have also omitted all cases of diffuse keratitis. At the same time I desire to state that I have never found descemetitis absent during the active period of this disease. Finally, before taking up the individual cases and conditions, I desire to state that the following notes are taken from my histories, many of which are unsatisfactory because incomplete, or because of the failure of patients to return.

A. CASES OF DESCEMETITIS WITHOUT OTHER DISEASE.

CASE 1.—Mr. G., aged 30, was seen July 3, 1900. The sight of the left eye was blurred and the eye had been painful for two weeks. The pupil responded promptly to atropia. There was marked descemetitis. Atropin was ordered. Two days later there was no evidence of iritis, and the fundus appeared normal.

CASE 2.—Miss R., white, aged 29, complained of her eye for

tically blind; yet, in spite of numerous atrophies she had normal central vision. It is also noteworthy that in but one of the eighteen cases were both eyes involved.

Of the seventeen cases without descemetitis syphilis was present in three, while a fourth showed typical foveal changes, though neither history nor other evidence pointed to systemic infection. In the three, periods of two, six and nine years had elapsed since the initial lesion; considerably beyond the usual time for

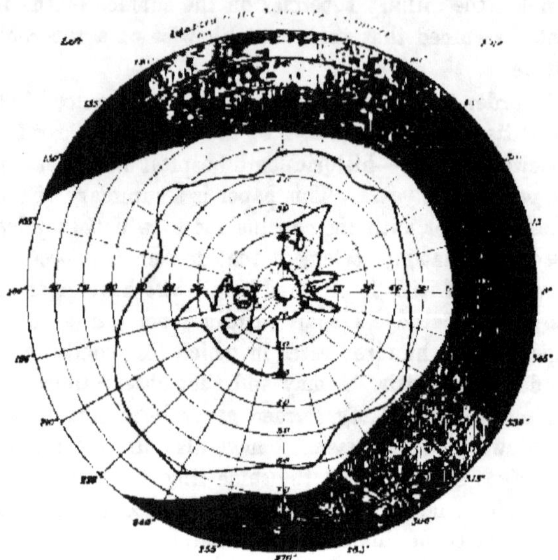

Fig. 3.—E and D. Shape of color scotomata and dim white areas.

secondary eye symptoms. Interesting queries are: how recent should infection be to justify causative relation, and, are the syphilitic foveal lesions sufficiently characteristic of this, in distinction to other forms, to justify diagnosis in absence of history or other manifestations? In these, in two cases of choroiditis disseminata and five with subretinal extravasations, visual impairment was confined to the field area corresponding to fundal lesion. Scotomata existed in eight, macropsia in one, photopsia in two; symptoms characteristic of choroidal disease. Causes, so far as determined, were syphilis in three, unknown in the fourth with specific changes, and gout in both cases of the disseminated variety. Hemorrhages occurred in two old patients who had atrophies, one during convalescence from pneumonia, a fourth in connection with severe asthenopia, the fifth coincident with menstrual suppression.

I shall use the remaining six patients as a basis for

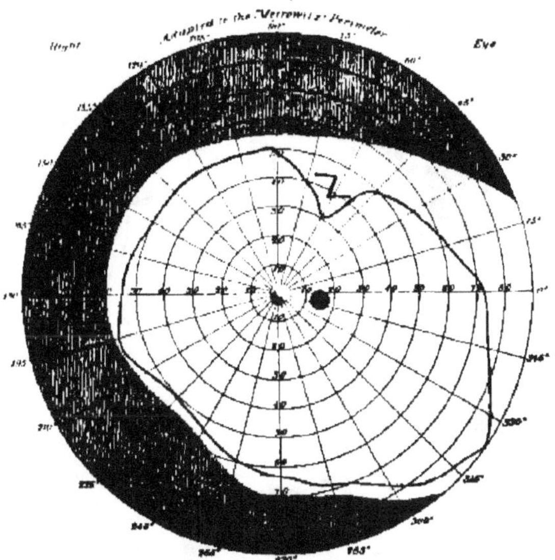

Fig. 4.—Narrowing of upper temporal field with decided "cut-in."

inquiry into the diagnostic and prognostic significance of the symptoms of so-called "choroidal hyperemia," and vitreous opacities. In Griffith's excellent article, already mentioned, the indefiniteness of symptoms of choroidal congestion is dwelt upon, reddened disc being practically the sole sign. This comes through cilio-retinal anastomosis. He says: "Even patches of localized inflammation may not be discoverable till they have broken through the hexagonal pigment layer of the re-

tina." Concerning vitreous opacities, he says: "They
are often absent through the entire course of the disease.
Their presence depends on the coincident implication
of the retina rather than upon the choroiditis itself,
and they are found only where the retinitis is more
marked than usual, and the inner layers are affected, as
shown by opacity of the retina and blurring of its vessels." He regards "the retinitis as a separate process,
from the same cause which produces the choroidal

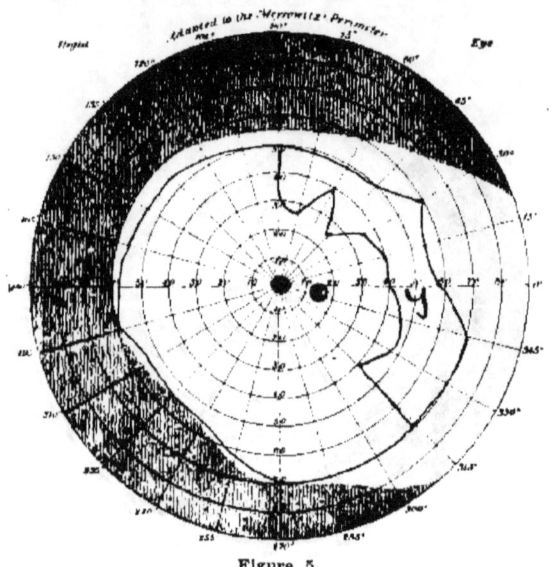

Figure 5.

trouble, and not as an extension of the latter." I can-
not resist the conviction that the statement concerning
vitreous opacities appearing only in connection with
opacity of the retina and blurring of its vessels will not
tally with general experience. I am sure I have seen
intensely red disc and muscæ without involvement of
retinal vessels. I have such a case now under observation: a lady 32 years old, with simple myopic astigmatism, normal central and peripheral vision. Red discs

and floating bodies were apparent on first examination
a year ago. Refraction correction seems to have re-
lieved the choroidal hyperemia, if such was the mean-
ing of the red disc; yet fine vitreous opacities are still
observable, and the eyes are not capable of prolonged
work. A boy of 19, student at Johns Hopkins Univer-
sity, whom I examined six years ago, had the same intra-
ocular appearances in an eye in which he had a positive
scotoma in the upper temporal field. Central vision was

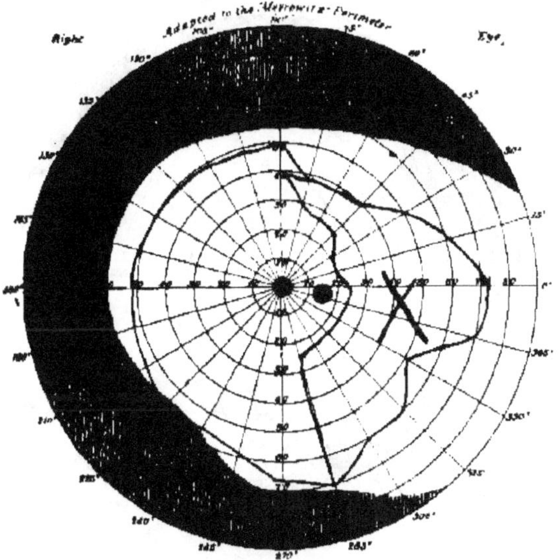

Figure 6.

unaffected. Symptoms had followed unusual eye work,
and recovery came after a few months' rest. I have had
under observation for ten years or so a lady in the
fifties who has persistently complained of muscæ in the
right eye. Central and peripheral vision have been normal. Several times have I noted this reddening of the
disc, and fine vitreous opacities when reviewing her
glasses. In March she came with a choroido-retinal
exudate. Some influence, apparently rheumatic, has

kept the eye sensitive and finally produced ophthalmoscopic choroido-retinitis.

In the following three cases changes followed each
other in such rapid succession as to leave no doubt that
the red disc and vitreous opacities meant serious trouble. A lady, 31 years of age, was seen in December,
1900, for defective central vision in the left eye. She
had consulted another oculist a month previous, who
had found choroiditis, and given an unfavorable prog-

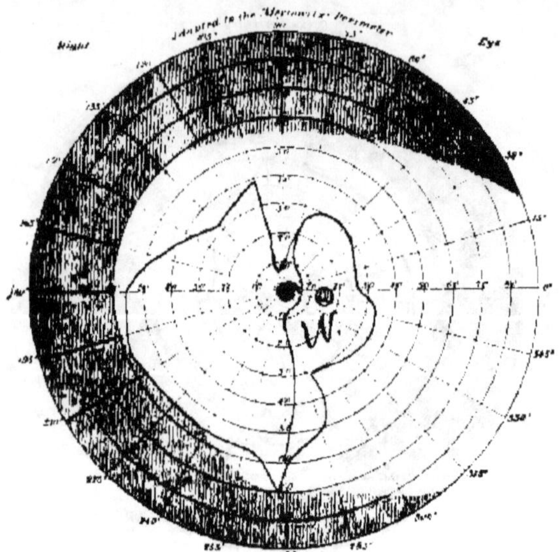

Figure 7.

Figs. 5, 6, 7 show progressive narrowing of right temporal field;
letters Y, X, W, color scotomata and dim white areas always preceding loss of portion of field.

nosis. Vision was 20/70, with a paracentral scotoma
(Fig. 1). Red disc, floating vitreous opacities and perifoveal pigment heaps were present. In eighteen months
fundal appearances have not materially changed. In
March, 1902, she thought this eye was getting worse.
Examination showed a peripheral positive scotoma and
two field areas in which colors were lost and white was

dence of lues. She was given red iodid of mercury alternating with iodid of potassium.

The patient has been seen frequently. This condition has fluctuated, but has not at any time disappeared. At the last examination on May 14, 1902, V-20/100. The right cornea is still studded with fine deposits. The lens is clear. The vitreous contains fine and coarse opacities. The fundus is normal and the field of vision for white and red is perfect. The left eye has not at any time shown any evidence of disease. Diagnosis: chronic cyclitis.

In the last series of cases there was sufficient evidence in the extensive vitreous opacities of deep uveitis, but as the fundus showed no abnormalities and the iris was unaffected, we place the lesion in the ciliary portion. The three cases that follow give still further evidence of uveitis in the development of cataract in young and otherwise healthy persons.

C. DESCEMETITIS WITH DEVELOPMENT OF CATARACT IN YOUNG PERSONS.

CASE 17.—Mrs. N., aged 32, was first seen Jan. 23, 1898. She complained of having had "spots before her sight" for some time, and that in the past few weeks the condition had become much worse. In the right eye there were numerous dust-like, vitreous opacities, and the lens likewise contained similar opacities. The optic disc and retina appeared normal. In the left eye there was rapidly developing cataract, and the fundus could not be examined. Both corneæ were studded with fine and coarse deposits. Close examination did not reveal any choroidal lesions even in the periphery. Vision in the right eye was 6/8, 6/6 partly with plus 1.5 Ds; the left eye distinguished fingers at four feet. The field of vision of both eyes (for white and colors), was approximately normal. The patient was carefully examined and was found healthy in every respect (heart, blood and urine). She was given iodid of potash in small doses, and later the red iodid of mercury. In March of the same year the vitreous of the right eye had become clearer, but there was still descemetitis in both eyes. The cataract of the left eye had increased. The descemetitis was discerned as late as April. In August I could find no deposits on the corneæ and the right vitreous was almost perfectly clear. The opacities in the right lens had not made any advance. There was at no time pain or other active signs of inflammation. The patient left the city and was not seen until December, 1899. The cataract in the left eye in the meantime became sufficiently mature to permit of an operation, which was performed Jan. 1, 1900. A small iridectomy was made

and an excellent result was obtained. The patient was last
seen in April, 1902. The vision of the left eye is perfect and a
careful examination of the fundus failed to reveal any changes.
The condition of the right eye is practically unchanged.

Case 18.—Miss F. D., aged 10, an apparently healthy and
well-developed girl, was first seen Feb. 3, 1898. She had complained for a few days of blurred vision in the right eye. The
right vitreous was filled with fine opacities. There was marked
descemetitis. No choroidal lesion could be found. The left
eye was perfectly normal. Vision was almost perfect. Toward
the end of the month the cornea became clearer. The patient
was seen frequently and on March 14, I observed a number of
small opacities near the posterior surface of the lens. They
gave the picture of minute bubbles. Vision remained about
the same and the field of vision was perfect. The corneal opacities were observed from time to time as late as November,
1899, but in April, 1900, the cornea was perfectly clear. In
the meantime the lenticular opacities had gradually increased
and formed a more or less circumscribed cataract in the outer,
upper portion of the posterior cortical layer. In October, 1901,
there was a recurrence of marked descemetitis and the opacity
of the lens had increased somewhat. She was last examined in
November, 1901, and numerous deposits were still found on
Descemet's membrane. The opacity of the lens had not increased and her vision is still good.

Case 19.—Mrs. G., aged 27, was seen on May 1, 1902. She
had been forced for the past few years to sew to an excessive
amount and had found that the sight of the left eye had been
failing. She was otherwise in good health, but had lost in
weight, which was due, as she thought, to overwork and worry.
The right eye was found to be perfectly normal (plus 1.75
V-6/5) ; left eye showed extensive descemetitis and opacities in
the form of small globules throughout the posterior portion of
the lens. The vitreous could not be examined, but a sufficiently
clear picture of the fundus was obtained to determine that the
optic disc was normal and that there were a few small, pale,
pink and sharply circumscribed spots in the periphery of the
choroid. The field of vision was slightly contracted.

The development of the cataract in these cases is the
expression of marked nutritive disturbance and can only
be ascribed to uveitis, for general constitutional disease
was definitely excluded. On the other hand, there were
in all the cases abundant opacities of the vitreous which
likewise indicated uveitis.

D. DESCEMETITIS ASSOCIATED WITH GLAUCOMA.

Case 20.—W. T., aged 42, was seen. July 24, 1900. There
was a deep glaucomatous excavation with atrophy of both pap-

illæ. The left fundus appeared blurred because of enormous vitreous opacities and gross descemetitis arranged in triangular form. Vision, right eye, 10/200, left eye, perception of light eccentric.

Case 21.—Mrs. F., aged 28, was seen April 10, 1902. Seven years before she had had trouble with the left eye, at first in the form of spots and after a time vision was entirely lost. The eye was never painful. She now suffered slight discomfort. T. plus ½ or 1. The pupil was not dilated. The cornea was studded with large deposits in the lower half, but the entire surface contained finer deposits. V=O. In order to exclude any malignant growth by ophthalmoscopic examination, a mydriatic was used in spite of the high tension. There was a cataractous opacity in the central posterior portion, but with the dilated pupil a dim image of the disc was seen. By parallactic movements the excavation was distinctly made out. No other fundus changes could be made out, but there were abundant vitreous opacities. The right eye was perfectly normal.

In the last two cases the evidence of uveitis are vitreous opacities, glaucoma and in the one cataract. The ophthalmoscopic image was not sufficiently distinct to exclude choroiditis with certainty.

E. DECEMETITIS WITH ACUTE CIRCUMSCRIBED EXUDATIVE CHOROIDITIS.

I have next to report that descemetitis was observed in 31 cases of fresh exudative choroiditis. These cases will not be detailed individually on this occasion. I shall reserve their publication for a separate paper, partly because it would require too much time, but especially because I am desirious of calling attention to many other points of interest in these cases besides descemetitis. This disease, which is observed between the ages of 17 and 50, the average age being 27¼, is characterized by the appearance of white or bluish white circumscribed effusions near the optic disc or the macula, but very frequently in the extreme periphery of the fundus. The size of the effusion mav be less than that of the disc or it may be six or eight times as large. The symptoms so far as vision is concerned consist most frequently in the appearance of muscæ with a blurring of central vision, which may be slight or marked, and result in complete loss of central vision when the effusion is in the foveal region. There is rarely any pain. I have examined in all 38 cases of this affection which were more or less recent and, as above stated, 31 showed descemetitis. In four, the patient was seen too late and the deposits had probably disappeared. In one the pupil was too small to make a careful examination, and in only two was there no explanation for their absence. Vitreous opacities were never absent. In many of these cases the corneal deposits disappeared within a few weeks, but the vitreous opacities lasted for a long time. The effusion gradually disappears and leaves an area of atrophy and irregular pigmentation. The disease shows marked tendency to recurrence.

I should like to say a word here as to how these effusions are to be found; the examination of the field of vision is an excellent guide, and has helped me in a number of cases. But I rely chiefly upon watching the ophthalmoscopic reflex in different portions of the fundus and examining with the indirect image whenever a whitish reflex appears.

F. DESCEMETITIS IN SYPHILITIC CHOROIDITIS.

Case 22.—Mr. H. was seen March 4, 1902. The patient had had luetic infection nineteen months before, followed by mucous patches, but without any skin eruption. An iritis in the left eye soon followed. This was rapidly cured. Eight months ago he noticed a scintillation before the left eye and vision dropped slightly. This scintillation has continued ever since and is very annoying. He does not complain of his right eye. In the left eye there are dense vitreous opacities, but the papilla can be made out with a little difficulty; the cornea is studded with descemetitis; there are numerous brown spots on the lens, traces of old iritis. The upper lid droops slightly. In the right eye the fundus appears normal, there are some vitreous opacities and fine descemetitis. Vision of the left eye scarcely 3/45. In the right 6/18. The patient was put on mercurial inunctions and jaborandi. He was last seen May 1. Vision had improved; right eye, 6/15, —0.75 Ds 6/9 almost; left eye 6/30, —0.5 Ds 6/15 partly. The fundus had cleared sufficiently to show a few light pinkish choroidal spots, typical of syphilitic choroiditis.

In this connection I desire to state that in another case under observation at the same time, in which but one eye was involved and the condition never became as bad as in that just described, no corneal deposits were observed.

I wish next to refer briefly to a few cases in which the chief disease appeared to be extra- and not intra-ocular. At the beginning of this paper I referred to diffuse keratitis. I have observed descemetitis twice in cases of circumscribed keratitis.

G. DESCEMETITIS ASSOCIATED WITH CIRCUMSCRIBED INTERSTITIAL KERATITIS.

CASE 23.—Mr. O., aged 25, was seen in April, 1896. There was circumscribed keratitis which at first appeared to be incipient diffuse keratitis, but which did not take this course. There was marked descemetitis. There are no notes as to the fundus.

CASE 24.—Mr. E., aged about 30, who was first seen Feb. 15, 1902, complaining of the left eye. He ascribed his trouble to having had a little hot wax fly into the eye, after which the eye had remained red for some time. There was no constitutional disease and lues was denied. When first seen there was slight injection of the eyeball just below the cornea, a small area of sclerotizing keratitis, fine descemetitis and the fundus was normal. He was seen again March 21, the fundus was normal and there were no signs of iritis; a few fine blood vessels had penetrated into the sclerotizing region, and there was still descemetitis. The patient had been seen in consultation with his family physician, who reported on May 1 that the eye had become perfectly normal.

H. DESCEMETITIS ASSOCIATED WITH SCLERITIS.

A second extra-ocular condition with which I have found descemetitis associated is scleritis.

CASE 25.—Thomas K., aged 27, had lues for two months, when he was attacked with severe scleritis. The fundus was perfectly normal. A week later there was fine descemetitis with numerous larger deposits. Two weeks after this the scleritis had disappeared (under specific treatment) and the cornea was much clearer.

CASE 26.—Mrs. B., aged about 35, had double retrobulbar optic neuritis in April, 1896, from which she recovered with very good vision. In January, 1899, she returned with inflammation of both eyes, which had made its appearance almost immediately after having exposed herself to the cold while menstruating (without any additional covering she hung out her wash on a very cold day). There was well-marked scleritis in both eyes. I left the city soon afterward and did not see her again till June, 1901. She had had the scleritis for a long time, but was now free. At this time there was marked descemetitis, especially in the right eye, without fundus changes.

In neither of the two cases just cited is there any note of uveitis. Scleritis frequently results in uveal involvement, and I am inclined to believe that there was secondary involvement of uveal tract in both of these cases. I have found iritis and old synechiæ in several of my cases of scleritis.

CONDITIONS IN WHICH DESCEMETITIS IS ABSENT.

I have not found descemetitis in any cases of disseminated choroiditis, central choroiditis, senile choroiditis, myopic choroiditis, and, as mentioned above, it was absent in one case of syphilitic choroiditis in which it was carefully looked for, and in several others in my case books. It is absent in hemorrhages of the retina, choroid or vitreous, and I have never seen it in any case of retinitis excepting in syphilitic retinitis (but in this case there was also iritis).

SUMMARY.

Keratitis punctata interna, or descemetitis, is observed in various ocular diseases. It is found in every case of iritis. It is an almost constant sign of exudative choroiditis and is sometimes found in syphilitic choroiditis. It is also observed in cases of acute and of chronic cyclitis. It is found in diffuse and in circumscribed keratitis, in which cases it probably depends upon an underlying uveitis. It is sometimes seen in scleritis; and is then probably due to associated, perhaps secondary, uveitis. When no other signs of uveal disease are noted besides descemetitis, as in the first three cases of our series, it is due to carelessness in the examination.

Excluding the cases of external disease (diffuse and circumscribed keratitis and scleritis) and the great category of iritis, I have been able to report on 53 cases. Even including those earlier ones in which the examinations were not made with the thoroughness of those of later years and including those in which the opacities of the media prevented examination of the fundus, they show that about three-fifths have exudative choroiditis. This ratio is indeed high; I ascribe it to the fact that, convinced for a number of years of the frequency of these cases, I have examined the fundus in many cases for a long time and repeatedly until I found the looked-for lesion. In some the diagnosis was not made until the second visit and after a mydriatic had been used, and in several of those seen in dispensary practice the lesion was not observed by any of those who examined the cases until it had been pointed out to them. Experience has taught me that a large number of these cases pass through the hands of skilled ophthalmologists without discovery of the true lesion. I do not hesitate to say that if my earlier cases had been examined more carefully exudative choroiditis would have appeared relatively still more frequent than has been shown in this paper. It is due to ignorance of these facts and to carelessness in examination that so many cases are still recorded as "serous iritis" and "serous cyclitis." It should be noted that we can examine with the ophthalmoscope only that part of the choroid lying back of the equator, and, at most, with a dilated pupil the equatorial region or a little beyond it.[2] Exudations in the anterior portion of the choroid may therefore be beyond the reach of the ophthalmoscopic examination. Such cases will be grouped with cyclitis.

Do the cases reported throw any light on the nature of the cyclitis with which descemetitis is associated? We know that descemetitis occurs in iritis, in which disease we always have an exudative inflammation. We find descemetitis in choroiditis only when there is exudative inflammation. It is but reasonable to infer on clinical grounds that descemetitis occurs in cyclitis only when there is exudative inflammation. The "serous iritis"

---

2. Hirschberg, Centralbl. f. Augenheilk., 1891, p. 324.

and "serous cyclitis" have, therefore, no clinical bases. That they have no pathological basis has been pointed out recently by Bruns.[3] It is to be hoped that these terms will be discarded in the future, and our section would do well to express itself with decision to this effect. One point that I should especially like to impress by my paper is, that in a large proportion of cases ordinarily diagnosed as "serous iritis" and "serous cyclitis" we find exudative choroiditis.

---

3. Archives of Ophthalmology, 1901, p. 569.

INJURIES OF THE EYE PRODUCTIVE OF DIS-
EASES OF THE UVEAL TRACT.

HOWARD F. HANSELL, M.D.
PHILADELPHIA.

The accidents to which the eye is exposed are mani-
fold. Notwithstanding its bony environment and its
soft and resilient orbital cushion, the prominent and
commanding position in the head affords a conspicuous
target for flying missiles, and the insufficient protec-
tion afforded by the lids and lashes and the practically
uninterrupted functional application of the eye during
working hours materially contribute to its dangers.
The fortunate provision of nature, the endowment of
man with two eyes, saves us from blindness should dis-
aster overtake one-half of the visual anatomy, but this
very duality multiplies the danger, and, more than that,
uncared traumatic inflammation of the one threatens
the safety of the other eye.

Apparently insignificant injuries are sometimes followed by the most disastrous results. This ocular in-
consistency between cause and effect is to be traced in
every instance to either delayed or unwise treatment or
to the state of the constitution of the individual at the
time the injury is received.

It seems to me useless to spend the time allotted to
the reading of this paper, or your time in listening to it,
by consideration of the kinds of injuries, such as in-
cisions, punctured wounds, concussion, foreign bodies,
etc., or to dwell on the well-known exceedingly complicated anatomy of the uveal tract and the diseases in-

duced by accidents. I prefer, therefore, to confine my remarks to a brief discussion of the constitutional complications and the early and late treatment of injuries of the eye causative of disease of the uveal tract.

The object of the treatment is two-fold, namely, the preservation of useful vision and, in cases in which this result is unobtainable, the saving of the eyeball.

A favorable prognosis depends in large measure, as I have intimated, on a constitution free from inherited or acquired taint and uncorrupted by devitalizing habits.

I wish to direct your attention to the pernicious influence on the course and termination of traumatic inflammation of syphilis, diabetes and tuberculosis. Any one of these affections will render the prognosis uncertain if not actually bad by intensifying the inflammation or changing its character, or developing a tendency to involve adjacent or remote organs.

SYPHILIS.

In syphilitic patients injuries to the eye are accompanied by exudation from the iris, ciliary body and choroid that destroys the transparency of the media and tends to alter the normal relation between secretion and excretion, and leads eventually to secondary degeneration. From the iris the exudation is poured into the anterior and posterior chamber and into the tissue of the iris, and from the posterior portion of the uveal tract into the vitreous. The iris becomes adherent on its posterior surface and pupillary border to the lens and the pupil occluded. Precautionary iridectomy is followed by further ·exudation and by closure of the coloboma, and finally the ball is enucleated to save the pain of secondary glaucoma. In view of this common termination the inception of traumatic iridocyclitis must be energetically combated by the free exhibition of mercury and the iodids, and the earlier this treatment is instituted the more hopeful the outcome. My experience leads me to believe that the most thorough and rapid method is by mercurial inunction or calomel in small and frequently repeated doses, combined with iodid of potassium in rapidly increasing amounts. Salivation and iodism are postponed and the influence of the remedies increased by the simultaneous institution of the sweat treatment by pilocarpin, hot baths and the usual adjuncts. Locally, the frequent use of strong solutions of atropia, hot compresses, leeches and blisters is indicated. The subconjunctival injections of large quantities of weak solutions of mercury bichlorid are reported to have been useful in checking inflammation and preventing suppuration. Their good offices I have witnessed in one striking case. A non-syphilitic boy of 3 was badly wounded by a rusty iron hinge. The cornea was torn through, the iris and probably the lens were prolapsed, and after a few days the ocular contents showed every indication of becoming purulent. Repeated injections of mercuric bichlorid, 1-10,000, under the conjunctiva saved the ball and made an iridectomy possible.

The general and constitutional symptoms of syphilis are in most cases sufficiently pronounced to enable one to determine the presence of this dyscrasia. For example, in the inherited form we have the facies syphilitica, the scarred mouth, the Hutchinson teeth, the enlarged glands or the scars of ulcerated and broken-down glands; in the acquired form, the history, the cutaneous stains, iritic synechiæ, chorio-retinitis, point unmistakably to the affection. When, however, there are no indications to be seen or learned, and when one must judge by the course of the inflammation following the injury for which the patient has come under treatment, one is guided by the amount of exudation disproportionate to the degree of inflammation, the nocturnal rather than the diurnal pain and its chronic course. I have not been able to determine that the danger of sympathetic inflammation is any greater in syphilitics than in non-syphilitics. It must be borne in mind in dealing with these cases in which iridocyclitis attacks the uninjured eye that it may be a manifestation of syphilis, developed, perhaps, in consequence of the injury and subsequent inflammation of the other eye for the same occult reason that acute glaucoma is lighted up in one eye after iridectomy on the other for glaucoma. Such accidents can not be attributed to sympathy, or, at least, to the affection of the second eye following traumatisms where the origin of that affection is derived undoubtedly from the traumatism and known as sympathetic ophthalmia. I feel very sure that some of the cases reported as sympathetic ophthalmia, and particularly those appearing weeks or months or years after enucleation are local manifestations in the hitherto sound eye of constitutional affections, with especial reference to syphilis.

DIABETES.

Injuries to the eyes of diabetics are almost invariably the cause of serious damage to, if not of the loss of, the eye. The truth of this statement can be abundantly verified. Those of us who have been careless in examining into the bodily condition before extracting a cataractous lens, or who have had the operation forced upon us, will agree they have had more failures than successes. The tendency of diabetics to gangrene is not more marked in any other portion of the body than in the eye, but fortunately the tendency becomes manifest only after injury. The uveal tract and the tissues that are dependent upon it for their health and growth give early indication of the blood impoverished by diabetes. Iritis, cataract, vitreous opacities and degeneration of choroid and retina in patches are common ocular complications of diabetes, and each of them is evidence of the disturbed nutrition. Now when an injury is the exciting cause of inflammation, the pre-existing tendency to involvement in the general affection will lead to results that are disastrous and entirely unwarranted by the character of the injury. For example, I have recently had under treatment a man who received on the cornea an apparently insignificant injury from impact of a small foreign body. The body was removed. The floor and edges of the wound became infiltrated with pus. In spite of the most active treatment, both for the abscess and the diabetes, the entire cornea was destroyed, exposing the iris and permitting of the escape of the lens and vitreous, necessitating finally enucleation. In another case preliminary iridectomy and massage of the lens for ripening of a cataract was followed by numerous hemorrhages into the anterior chamber, chronic iridocyclitis and loss of the eye.

We learn from these and similar cases: 1, the necessity for the examination of the urine for sugar preparatory to the operation for the extraction of cataract; 2, the obligation to consider all cases of injury serious until they are proven slight; 3, the necessity for strict remedial and dietetic measures in diabetes mellitus, and 4, in spite of treatment an unfavorable prognosis.

TUBERCULOSIS.

In individuals with a predisposition to tubercle, injuries to the eye, and particularly the penetration through the coats of cutting instruments or of foreign bodies, may give rise to local tuberculosis. This is brought about by one of two influences, namely, either the entrance with the foreign body of the tubercle bacillus or the stimulation to activity of bacilli pre-existing in a latent form at the site of the injury. The uveal tract and the contents of the vitreous and aqueous chamber furnish fertile soil for the multiplication of bacteria. Their growth is rapid, and equally rapid is the destruction of the function of the ball. The eye is destroyed by chronic iridocyclitis that is not amenable to treatment. As soon as the diagnosis is established by inoculation of part of the contents of the eye into the eye of one of the lower animals the ball should be enucleated. This is imperative. Delay will mean that the infection will become general and end in the death of the patient. We must expect similar processes of inflammation and disease to follow traumatism to the eye that are familiar in other parts of the body after injuries. Scrofula, which, in the opinion of some writers, is an hereditary form of diluted tuberculosis, is a predisposing cause to tardy healing of wounds, and should not be overlooked in the examination to determine the constitutional reason for chronic forms of inflammation after traumatism.

Early enucleation of a badly injured eye saves the patient and the surgeon annoyance and time, and has become, I think, a fashion. The patient's confidence in his physician must not be betrayed, and the most convincing argument in favor of enucleation, namely, the fear of sympathetic inflammation, should not be abused. One must be convinced beyond the shadow of a doubt that vision is irretrievably ruined before resorting to extreme measures. Nature's recuperative powers combined with human knowledge and antiseptic remedies accomplish wonderful cures. And sympathetic inflammation is not always as black as it is painted. It never follows immediately after the injury, it always gives warning and it may never come. I except from these rules eyes that contain a foreign body that can not be extracted. In the cases of foreign body in which the ciliary region is the site of the injury, or likely to become irritated by the presence of the body in the eye, immediate enucleation is the only safe treatment. The presence of a foreign body is indicated by chronic or recurrent intractable inflammation of the uveal tract. Sympathetic inflammation will supervene in three weeks or later, and can be prevented only by the extraction of the foreign substance or removal of the eye. There ought to be no uncertainty in the diagnosis, for unless the foreign substance is extremely small the x-rays will determine beyond reasonable doubt its presence. In all other classes of injury unless the traumatism is unusually destructive the expectant plan of treatment should be adopted and enucleation reserved as the last resort.

CONCLUSIONS.

1. Injuries to the ciliary zone are always serious and often destructive of the usefulness of the eye.

2. The syphilitic, diabetic or tubercular diathesis delays recovery and renders the prognosis uncertain.

3. Diseases of the uveal tract the result of injuries are favorably modified by the energetic treatment of these constitutional affections.

4. Enucleation or one of its substitute operations is to be practiced immediately when a foreign body lies embedded in the ciliary region and can not be extracted, or when an eye is mangled beyond hope of redemption.

5. Conservative measures, such as cold compresses, antiseptic washes, subconjunctival injections, excision of prolapsed iris or ciliary body, rest in bed, restricted diet, morphia and other means to subdue inflammation should be the rule in other cases.

PATHOLOGY OF UVEITIS.

WILLIAM H. WILDER, M.D.

Assistant Professor of Ophthalmology, Rush Medical College; Professor of Ophthalmology, Chicago Policlinic; Surgeon and Pathologist, Illinois Charitable Eye and Ear Infirmary.

CHICAGO.

Properly speaking, the term uveitis should be applied to an inflammation of any portion of the uveal tract which embraces iris, ciliary body and choroid; and an inflammatory process in any one of these structures, if severe and protracted, may involve the other divisions. Hence we frequently have cyclitis and choroiditis associated with severe iritis, if not caused by it, and likewise in suppurative choroiditis and even in certain types of protracted plastic choroiditis the iris and ciliary body become affected.

Thinking it better to limit the subject, this paper will consider particularly lesions of the choroid.

CLASSIFICATION.

A satisfactory pathologic classification of the forms of choroiditis is difficult, for although we recognize that these forms differ as to their etiology, the situations of their lesions, and their clinical appearances, yet their pathologic anatomy is by no means so varied. However, the usual division into purulent or suppurative choroiditis and plastic choroiditis seems a simple and convenient one. Whether or not we should add to this a third division, namely, serous, to explain some of the insidious, slow forms that so frequently have associated with them so-called serous inflammation of the ciliary

body and iris, together with slight changes in the vitreous, is a question. It would seem to be simpler to
omit this and consider them all as belonging to one of
the two divisions, suppurative or plastic. Undoubtedly
the liability of this part of the uveal tract to any form
of inflammation is largely due to the extraordinary rich-
ness of its capillary system, which even exceeds that of
the alveoli of the lung. It is estimated by Vierordt and
by Wedl and Bock that the blood current of the chorio-
capillaris as compared with the arteries that supply it
is enlarged more than thirty-two times, and in consequence of this the current is markedly reduced, both in
velocity and strength. Every active hyperemia of the
arteries and every passive congestion of the veins of
the eye must make itself felt in the increased tension
of the choroid. Again, should there be any change in
the tunica intima or the vessel walls because of the circulation in the blood of any deleterious substance, this
slowing of the current would encourage the heaping up
of leucocytes on the walls and diapedesis into the tissue outside the vessels. This peculiarly bountiful arrangement of the vessels must be an important factor
in the pathology of the choroid, and we can understand
why many of the lesions have their beginning in the
innermost layers.

THE SUPPURATIVE FORM.

In acute suppurative choroiditis there is at first a rapid
infiltration of the vascular layers of the choroid with
round cells. The vessels become blocked with emboli
and thrombi. The external layers and the supracho-
roidal space are distended by a fibrinous exudation. The
accumulation of pus cells beneath the lamina vitrea lifts
up the retina, which soon becomes involved in the inflammatory process and its elements break down. The
vitreous becomes turbid. Intraocular pressure is increased. As the severity of the inflammation increases
the infiltration works its way forward to the ciliary
body and the iris. Exudate appears in the anterior

chamber. Marked congestion of the anterior ciliary veins occurs because of the interference of the circulation, and pronounced edema of the conjunctiva, orbital tissues and even the lids results, giving us the well-known appearances of panophthalmitis. The tissue of the sclerotic coat may become infiltrated and softened and by rupturing allow the escape of the purulent, disintegrated contents of the globe. Usually, however, it is the cornea that first gives way. The organization of inflammatory products beneath the capsule of Tenon attach it firmly to the sclerotic and obliterate Tenon's space, and masses of new, firm connective tissue develop around the eyeball. The disease is a septic one and usually some variety of the pus formers may be demonstrated.

Most of the cases are of traumatic origin, but in some of them the infection may be metatastic, as in postpartum choroiditis coming on as a result of puerperal septicemia, which frequently proves fatal. In these cases bacterial emboli in the choroidal vessels or even in the retinal vessels are the starting point of the .rapidly destructive inflammation. These cases are frequently associated with ulcerative endocarditis and multiple abscesses in other organs. A form of suppurative choroiditis, probably metastatic in origin, running a sluggish course and not resulting in destruction of the eye, is known as pseudo-glioma. It occurs in very young children, usually under three years of age. There is usually a history of preceding meningitis or of bronchitis or some exanthematous disease. In one case I saw the trouble follow an attack of mumps. The vitreous chamber fills up with a mass of exudate, which may be seen through the pupil lying up against the back part of the lens. The retina may or may not be detached. The choroid is thickened and sometimes shows thrombosis of the vessels and hemorrhages into its substance. In other cases no marked lesion of the choroid is present and the exudate seems to come from the ciliary body. These eyes are frequently removed with a diagnosis of glioma.

PLASTIC CHOROIDITIS.

In considering the clinical forms of plastic or non-suppurative choroiditis, most authors describe them under the headings, disseminated choroiditis, areolar choroiditis, central choroiditis, choroido-retinitis and anterior and posterior sclero-choroiditis. While the different situation of the lesions and the varied ophthalmoscopic appearance make it possible to differentiate these forms clinically, so far as their pathologic anatomy is concerned, at least of the disseminated, areolar and central forms, they are very similar. Examination of such a choroidal lesion at the beginning, will show the capillaries enlarged and surrounded with leucocytes These round cells, together with amorphous fibrinous exudation, become heaped up in a mass in the layer of the chorio-capillaris beneath the vitreous membrane, which may be slightly raised by the pressure of the exudate. The capillaries are engorged with blood. The pigment layer of the retina remains intact. Seen with the ophthalmoscope at this stage, this mass may look like a small yellowish-red patch, not raised above the surface of the choroid. Such patches are at first discrete, but contiguous ones may coalesce to form larger patches of more irregular shape. As the case progresses these exudation masses are either absorbed or undergo in part organization, so that new cicatricial tissue takes the place of the mass of exudate, and the choroidal tissue atrophies. The elements of the pigment layer of the retina now proliferate, the layer of rods and cones is destroyed and pigment masses may be found in the outer layers of the retina itself, as well as in the margins of the choroidal area because of the proliferation of the pigment cells of the choroidal stroma. In the severer cases the retina becomes adherent to the atrophic cicatricial patches by the growth of the radial fibers outward into the choroid, so that a depressed cicatrix of the retina and choroid results. This cicatricial tissue in the choroid is illustrated in a case that recently came under my observation.

NARRATION OF CASE 1.

CASE 1.—John L., a strong, healthy young farmer, 22 years old, was seen by me in March of this year. The only illness of any note in the personal history was typhoid six years ago. No history of syphilis or rheumatism.

Eighteen months before I first saw him, without any assignable cause, his vision failed rapidly so that in thirty-six

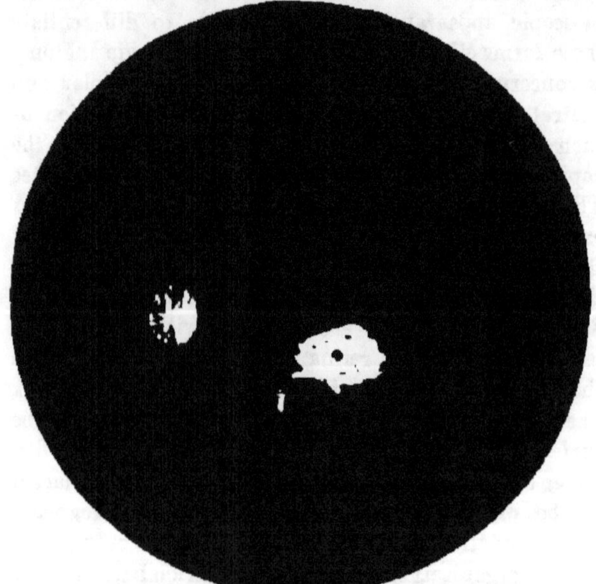

Case 1.—John L. Left eye. Erect image.

hours after the onset he stated he was unable to read. Then vision gradually improved so that when first seen by me, R. V.=20/200; L. V.=20/50. There was a central choroiditis in each eye with irregular patches of choroidal atrophy and whitish masses of new connective tissue in the choroid with masses of pigment interspersed.

He was put on large doses of iodid of potassium and at the time of his discharge, May 29, 1902, R. V.=20/50; L. V.=20/20. The condition of the fundus is shown in the drawing, for which I am indebted to Dr. Chas. H. Beard of Chicago.

The vitreous becomes cloudy from small particles of exudate and round cells that find their way into it. At this stage the ophthalmoscopic appearance is pronounced. Larger or small irregularly-shaped whitish patches more or less completely surrounded by black borders, interspersed between which are irregular masses of pigment scattered throughout the choroid, make up the picture of disseminated choroiditis. The peripheral portions of the fundus may be most affected, or this may be free, and the posterior central part may be the seat of the lesion.

The form described by Förster as areolar choroiditis differs in no way from the preceding, pathologically. The mass is made up of cellular elements aggregated in a thickened choroid. There is, however, a proliferation of the pigment layer of the retina, so that with the ophthalmoscope there seems to be at first merely a round or oval mass of pigment. Gradually, with the absorption of the exudate, there is seen the characteristic circular atrophic area surrounded by a ring of pigment.

The diseased patch is sharply differentiated from the normal choroid. The posterior pole of the eye is the part preferably selected, although the region of the yellow spot may escape for a considerable time, it may be years, to be suddenly involved. In consequence of this, central vision may remain good, although perimetric examination of the field will reveal numerous scotomata corresponding to the site of the choroidal lesions.

It is more than probable that the outer layers of the retina derive their nourishment from the capillary layer of the choroid, and for this reason, inflammatory processes in the latter often involve the retina.

We may have a diffuse or a circumscribed choroido-retinitis and, if the region of the macula is the part particularly affected, the term central choroido-retinitis is applicable.

The pathologic process in these cases is similar and consists in a parenchymatous infiltration of the choroid,

which later involves the retina, causing a destruction
of the pigment and bacillary layers. Degeneration of
the connective tissue of the retinal layers follows, and
atrophy of this structure. Immigration of pigment is
noticeable in surrounding areas of the retina, this pigment being arranged along the retinal vessels, but not
covering them as in pigmentary degeneration of the
retina (retinitis pigmentosa). Opacities, at first small,
dust-like spots, later larger masses, are seen in the posterior part of the vitreous and obscure the optic disc
and vessels. These are more marked in the diffuse form
and are said to be always present in the syphilitic form
of the disease and to be one of the earliest signs.

According to Schöbl, the vessel walls are thickened
sometimes to the extent of obliteration of the lumen,
and evidences of endarteritis exist in marked swelling
of the tunica intima. Ophthalmoscopically the retinal
vessels are seen to be markedly narrowed and in places
obliterated. The appearances vary according to the
situation of the lesions, the intensity of the inflammation, the stage of the disease and the presence or
absence of proliferation in the choroid. A case of
central choroido-retinitis that has been under observation for three years, in which there is absolutely no history of syphilis, passed through this course and has re-
sulted in almost total loss of central vision.

NARRATION OF CASE 2.

CASE 2.—Mrs. W., aged 46 years, was first examined by me
April 4, 1896. She had slight hyperopic astigmatism in each
eye, the correction of which gave normal vision. Media and
fundus at the time were normal. Somewhat more than one
year later she noticed dimness of vision of left eye, and examination revealed the faintest possible opacities of the vitreous
which reduced the vision to 20/30. No change in the fundus.
One year later these opacities had somewhat increased and a
slight grayish appearance of the fovea was noticed. Vision in
that eye had fallen to 20/50. Two months later L. V.=20/100
and the grayish spot exactly in the fovea had grown a little
larger. The trouble gradually increased until one year later,
Jan. 10, 1900, L. V.=20/200. The vitreous opacities were no
more numerous, but there was more change in the yellow spot

region. From this time on the central vision became more and more impaired until it reached zero, while the fundus assumed the appearance shown in the drawing, which was made a few days ago.

The patient had some rheumatic or gouty tendencies, not well-marked, however, and was passing through the menopause. The right eye has remained normal.

SCLERO-CHOROIDITIS.

On the edges of the conus found in high degrees of

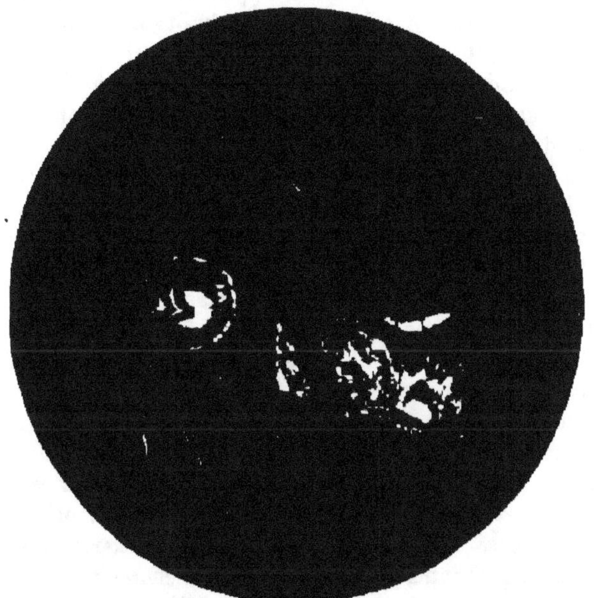

Case 2.—Mrs. W. Left eye. Erect image. Drawn May 25, 1902.

progressive myopia are found distinct signs of inflammation of the choroid. There is a proliferation of the pigment cells on the edge of the affected area and the pigment is heaped up in masses. The capillaries are closed and even disappear. There is an infiltration into the layers of the choroid and even into the sclerotic, the fibers of which become atrophied, so that because of the thinning of the sclera, ectasia may occur. The epithelial cells of the retina disappear over the conus and the layer of rods and cones is not seen over this area.

With the increase of the myopia the atrophy extends to the nasal side of the optic disc and forms a complete ring around it. In advanced cases the changes about the yellow spot speak for an inflammatory condition. Numerous whitish lines and spots of exudate, together with small hemorrhages, are sometimes seen.

Schnabel contends that the appearances of the conus in high degrees of myopia are not due to inflammatory changes, but that they are congenital defects. According to this author, the bacillary and pigment layers were never formed over the area of the conus, and so could not be drawn away.

I have several times observed cases of localized choroiditis with descemetitis similar to the anomalous forms described by Hill Griffith. In these there was dimness of vision coming on suddenly. Examination showed distinct spots on the posterior surface of the cornea, but there were no signs of iritis or irido-cyclitis. In other cases, however, there were iritic complications and also dust-like opacities in the vitreous, so that I am inclined to believe that in most cases where descemetitis is present there is some involvement of the anterior part of the uveal tract. In both choroido-retinitis and central choroiditis I have observed that opacities of the vitreous, so faint as to escape a hurried examination without mydriatic, precede the manifest choroidal lesion, even in cases that are clearly nonsyphilitic.

THE TREATMENT OF CERTAIN NON-SPECIFIC LESIONS OF THE UVEAL TRACT WITH PILOCARPIN AND SWEAT BATHS.

THOMAS A. WOODRUFF, M.D.
CHICAGO.

The pilocarpin sweat is by no means new in the treatment of diseases of the eye. About 1877-78 we first find mention made of its having been successfully used in various inflammatory affections of the interior of the eyeball. Since that date the literature of the subject is quite extensive. Several authorities, among whom may be mentioned De Wecker and De Grandmont, early recommended its use for the absorption of opacities in the vitreous and of inflammatory products in the choroid. During the succeeding years we find a number of articles contributed by men of good repute who speak highly of the use of the drug, not only in the diseases of the uveal tract, but in detachment of the retina and in optic neuritis and reports of cases in which marked benefit has been derived from its use. While in some cases the pilocarpin was given by the mouth, the majority of observers prefer its hypodermatic administration. In some cases the drug was used alone, while in others it was used in conjunction with mercurial inunctions, potassium iodid, etc., and then without particular regard to the character—specific or other—of the intra-ocular lesion.

THE SCOPE OF THIS ARTICLE.

It is not the purpose of this paper to advocate anything new, but once more to draw the attention of this section to a valuable method of treating certain diseases of the uveal tract that seems to have fallen into desuetude. I shall confine my remarks to a consideration of certain affections of the posterior segment of the eyeball, and shall describe that method of employing it which, in my hands, has been followed by good results, not only in bringing to a standstill the degenerative process that has been going on, but in a number of cases clearing up the inflammatory products and restoring the tissues involved to a normal or nearly normal condition. Although disturbance of the general health is a frequent cause of non-specific lesions of the uvea, the patient giving a history of tuberculosis, anemia, etc., in many instances the chief etiologic factors are shrouded in mystery, the product of infection, when it is due to an infective process, being probably carried by the blood vessels. Although the uveal tract is abundantly supplied with blood vessels, the circulation is at the same time very sluggish and there is probably no other part of the body so prone to inflammatory and degenerative changes.

TECHNIC OF THE SWEAT BATH.

Many lesions of the choroid and ciliary body are in their nature irreparable, but a large minority are capable of some improvement. Notwithstanding the claims of many recent remedies, for example, the internal administration of thiosinamin, subconjunctival injections of mercury, etc., none of them give as good results in selected cases as the judicious use of the hypodermic injection of pilocarpin hydrochlorate in doses of one-eighth to one-quarter of a grain in conjunction with the sweat bath and the internal administration of potassium iodid. The iodid should be given in increasing doses in a large quantity of water until toxic symptoms appear. Although pilocarpin is by no means a new remedy, yet sufficient emphasis has not been placed upon its extreme value in certain deep lesions of the eye. Especially is this true in subacute and chronic choroiditis, hyalitis and opacities in the vitreous.

As the hypodermics and baths should be given when the stomach is empty, there being less danger from the untoward effects of pilocarpin at that time, they are best administered the first thing in the morning. The patient should be in bed and wrapped up to the neck in a blanket and again covered with at least four blankets. Under the latter half a dozen quart bottles containing boiling hot water should be placed. The hypodermic injection of pilocarpin hydrochlorate beginning with one-eighth of a grain should now be given, at the same time having the patient drink at least a pint of hot water, weak lemonade or tea. In a few minutes the patient should begin to break out into a profuse perspiration, which should continue for at least two hours, only stopping short of that time if he shows any bad symptoms. At the end of the sweat he should be thoroughly dried and the skin rubbed with alcohol and then allowed to rest the remainder of the day. This treatment should be continued at least every other day until twelve such baths are taken. At an interval of two or three weeks a similar course of treatment should be repeated, and then continued at various intervals as long as any improvement takes place.

INDICATIONS FOR USE.

In choroiditis, particularly of the exudative variety, I have found the administration of pilocarpin sweats very useful in the early stages before there is any involvement of the retinal elements and before the choroidal pigment has become absorbed. The drug seems to have a beneficial influence in the resorption of the choroidal exudates and allowing the affected tissues to resume their activity. In the more advanced stages of the disease where choroidal atrophy has already taken place, very little improvement of vision can be expected, but even in such cases the further progress of the disease may be checked and the patient retain useful vision. I think under such a course of treatment, before the choroid has been destroyed by atrophy, that we can safely encourage the patient in the hope of a favorable termination of his symptoms.

In vitreous opacities the results I have obtained in a number of cases by such a treatment in producing absorption of the opacities and clearing up of the vitreous have been very gratifying. In the recent cases where the opacities are small, although the vitreous may be so cloudy that the details of the fundus are made out with difficulty and visual acuity is very much lowered, there is usually a rapid clearing up of the exudates and visual acuity, if not fully restored to normal, may be greatly improved, so that useful vision is obtained. In cases of long standing and where the opacities appear as large, dark, irregular masses, the degeneration has been too extensive to expect much improvement from any treatment, and in such cases the prognosis is less favorable. Even in the recent cases the prognosis is not so favorable in those cases occurring in elderly people, still the progress of degeneration may be checked and absorption of a considerable portion of the exudate take place with retention of a useful amount of visual acuity. It is in the young individual where most favorable results are to be looked for.

In hemorrhage into the vitreous the prognosis is much more favorable where the extravasations are small, in which case complete absorption may take place. In the larger hemorrhages more permanent opacities are apt to remain in spite of treatment.

PRECAUTIONS TO BE TAKEN.

I am not in favor of pushing the drug until its physiologic effect is obtained. The disadvantages that are liable to arise from such a procedure are apt to offset any advantages we are getting from the drug, as the treatment may have to be discontinued and can not be returned to for several days. It is important that the treatment should be carried out systematically and

at regular intervals if we desire to get results. If
sweating is not produced satisfactorily from the first
dose, it is well to begin with not more than an eighth of
a grain; it can be judiciously increased until the dosage
is reached which produces a profuse sweating. I have
found that an eighth of a grain is quite sufficient in the
majority of instances, although I do not hesitate to give
larger doses when necessary. As yet I have not seen
any bad effects from the treatment as outlined, although
as high as a quarter of a grain of the drug has been used
on alternate days for several weeks at a time. I consider its administration subcutaneously more efficacious
than when given by the mouth.

ILLUSTRATIVE CASES.

CASE 1.—Mrs. J. B., aged 40, first seen Nov. 23, 1901, had
foggy vision in front of right eye with left half of objects more
blurred than the right half and could see wavy vertical lines
in front more marked toward the left half of vision.
R. V.=20/30 — J. viii and with glasses (105 + 0.50 + 0.75)
R. V.=20/15 and words J. ii. Some difficulty in distinguish-
ing colors. Field of vision showed a relative central scotoma
and several absolute scotomata scattered over lower portion
of field. Fields for color absent. No specific history. The
ophthalmoscope revealed a fine hyalitis with several small
partially movable vitreous opacities at the upper inner quad-
rant of the vitreous near the posterior surface of the lens.
Although there were no gross changes in the fundus a number
of small choroidal exudates could be seen situated between
optic disc and the macula.

Treatment.—Hypodermic injections of pilocarpin hydrochlorate one-eight grain with increasing doses of a saturated
solution of potassium iodid considerably cleared up the choroidal exudation and caused the vitreous opacities to disappear
entirely. The scotomata cleared and the field for colors,
although contracted, reappeared. In February she had a return of the symptoms but no vitreous opacities, although the
choroidal exudates could be distinctly seen and the field of
vision showed almost a complete absolute ring scotoma with
slight blurring at fixation point. A smaller course of treatment was undergone and after taking twelve of the sweats
there remained only a slight blurring where the absolute scotoma had been. Her condition since then has gradually improved and her eye feels very comfortable.

CASE 2.—Mrs. C. S. B., aged 26, L. E. chorioretinitis with
patches of choroidal atrophy in macular region and floating

vitreous opacities. R. E. choroidal exudates and pigmented patches of choroidal atrophy in periphery. L. V.=20/200; R. V.=20/20.

Treatment.—Pilocarpin sweats on alternative days for one month. Vision in left eye gradually improved until at end of one month L. V.=20/30. No potassium iodid given in this case.

CASE 3.—Henry W., aged 35. Myopic 7 D. in left and 5 D. in right eye. L. V. with glasses =20/40. R. V. with glasses =20/30. Ring-shaped spot in front left eye. In left eye has exudative choroiditis with floating membranous opacities. Right eye chronic choroiditis of myopic type.

Treatment.—Pilocarpin sweats. One-eighth grain increased to one-quarter grain, given for cne month with marked improvement in symptoms. Less vitreous opacities in left eye; vision much clearer. L. V.=20/30; R. V.=20/20. At same time taking increasing doses of saturated solution of potassium iodid as high as grs. 240 which was continued with intervals of rest after the sweats were stopped. At present V. with glasses =20/20.

CASE 4.—M. Q., aged 45, first noticed blurring in front of right eye followed by severe frontal headaches. Eyes ache and get red; sharp shooting pains through right eye. Gets dizzy during the day and staggers. The right eye hurts when moved in any direction, especially upward. L. V.=20/30 — J. i slowly. R. V.=20/70 — J. ii unimproved with glasses. Right eye: ophthalmoscope showed a hyalitis with dark cobwebby opacities in the vitreous. The details of the fundus could be made out with difficulty when irregular whitish patches could be seen in the macular regicn. Left eye: numerous choroidal exudates, especially to the nasal side of the optic disc. No vitreous opacities and media clear. Field of vision contracted in both eyes with a central blurring in field of right eye.

Treatment.—Pilocarpin sweats one-eighth grain increasing to one-sixth grain and increasing doses of saturated solution of potassium iodid. In ten days the headache, pain and soreness in right eye had become much less. L. V.=20/20 — J. i; R. V.=20/50 J. viii. The vitreous opacities were smaller and less numerous and the details of the fundus were better seen. At the end of one month: L. V.=20/15 J. i; R. V.=20/40 — J. iv. No vertigo, no headaches and no soreness on moving the right eye. The field of vision is only slightly contracted and the central scotoma has entirely disappeared from field of right eye. The vitreous still contains a few floating opacities and the fundus still shows some choroidal changes.

CASE 5.—Miss G. L., aged 17. Right eye: iridocyclitis, choroiditis. No details of the fundus can be made out on account of the floating opacities in the vitreous. Keratitis punctata. R. V. — fingers at 3 feet.

Treatment.—The iritis was treated with atropin, hot applications and dionin. After the acute stage of the iritis had subsided a course of pilocarpin sweats on alternate days was given hypodermically and saturated solution of potassium iodid in increasing doses, administered internally. At the end of twelve sweats the vitreous was much clearer and a hazy view of the fundus could be obtained, when a number of choroidal exudates scattered over the fundus could be seen. There were also fewer exudates on Descemet's membrane. R. V.=20/40. After an interval of three weeks the pilocarpin and potassium iodid were again given, the former on alternate days. After ten sweats had been taken the ophthalmoscope showed there were still present some faint opacities in the vitreous but less dense than formerly. The fundus could be seen distinctly, having a number of choroidal exudates scattered over it but no gross changes were present. The deposits on the posterior surface of the cornea had entirely disappeared. R. V.=20/30 — J. i.

THE TREATMENT OF UVEITIS.

WILBUR B. MARPLE, M.D.

NEW YORK CITY.

In considering briefly the subject of the "Treatment
of Uveitis," the author wishes first of all to disclaim, as
he did several months ago to our distinguished chair-
man, any intention of offering anything new or original
in the therapeutics of this condition. In the limits of
a paper like the present one we will have to content
ourselves often with very brief references to some methods of treatment, while to others no allusion at all can be
made.

After having tried various remedial agents suggested
at different times by numerous observers, and too often,
alas, with indifferent or no success, I must confess that
I am becoming less and less inclined to use with any degree of confidence the many new drugs of whose curative
powers we read such marvelous accounts. In many
instances I do feel it my duty to give them a trial on
some of our clinical patients; in many others, again,
the reports are so weird and improbable, or the reputa-
tion of the reporter for accuracy of observation is so
poor, that it has not seemed worth the trouble to try the
remedies even on our hospital patients. I find myself,
consequently, more and more disposed to fall back on a
few tried and trusty remedies, whose possibilities (as
I have discovered many a time) I had not by any means
exhausted.

Before undertaking the treatment of a case of uveitis
(or, for that matter, of anything else), our first and

most important task is to discover, if possible, what is
the underlying cause of the disease; what Mauthner
would call "die etiologische momente der zweiten Kate-
gorie," and from this get the indication for treatment.
In not a few cases our success in treating the ocular condition will depend largely upon our success in discover-
ing the underlying cause, whether it be syphilis, rheumatism, gout, influenza, malarial infection or any one
of numerous other causes, and directing our treatment
first of all to this.

The various papers on uveitis which have been read
to-day show that the subject has taken a very wide
range. While the iris is a part of the uveal tract, and
while an inflammation of this structure might be in-
cluded under the term uveitis, there is only one point
in the treatment of this disease to which I shall allude
to-day, and that is merely a word as to the treatment
of specific iritis. In my experience the great majority
of the cases of specific plastic iritis are early secondary
lesions and require the same treatment as other early
secondary syphilides, viz., mercury. My only excuse
for referring to this matter is that I have seen so many
cases of this disease in which iodids or mixed treatment
had been prescribed by other men generally considered
good ophthalmologists. In most of these cases, it seems
to me, that there is no indication whatever for the use
of the iodids.

The observation of Snellen[1] is doubtless familiar to
you all. In a case of so-called iritis serosa with increased tension he did a sclerotomy and one of the
small masses of exudate on the posterior surfaces of
the cornea came out, and when examined microscop-
ically was found to be, not a cluster of cells, but a col-
lection of microbes, very short bacilli. In a second
case he found cells, and between these he found microbes
similar to those found in the first case. From these observations he concludes that descemetitis is sometimes a
disease, *sui generis,* due to microbes whose toxins

6

cause irritation of the uveal tract. While this observation of Snellen would tend to show, therefore, that the condition may be at times a disease, *sui generis,* it is generally admitted that in most cases punctate keratitis or descemetitis is not a disease, but merely a symptom, perhaps of a process which long since ran its course.

Some months ago there was a man who made the rounds of the different eye clinics of New York City who presented this one symptom (of dots on Descemet's membrane) to as marked a degree as I have ever seen it. There was no redness or sensitiveness of the eye or any evidence of any acute process, and there was comparatively little visual disturbance, only numbers of unusually large dots on the posterior surface of the cornea, most numerous below, and evidently the remains of an old process, as they were absolutely unchanged during the period he was under observation, which was several months. Such a case, however, is unusual, for generally after the process is at an end the exudation or dots on the cornea disappear.

Recently I saw a case at the New York Eye Infirmary where the symptoms of punctate keratitis at once established the diagnosis, and consequently the treatment. The patient, a young hostler, complained of defective vision of only a few days' duration, and was turned over to an assistant for examination. The case was a very recent one, the media (with one exception, subsequently to be noted) were perfectly clear, and there was an opaque area at the macula with just a faint suggestion of redness at the center, and the assistant, who was not by any means a novice, made the diagnosis of embolism of the central artery of the retina, a condition to which on superficial examination it did have considerable resemblance. But more careful examination with dilated pupil disclosed, however, numerous dots on Descemet's membrane, especially below. As soon as the assistant's attention was called to this feature of the case he appreciated at once its significance, and that it established the existence of some inflammation of the uveal tract and promptly revised the diagnosis to that of choroidal exudation at the macula. Located as it was the visual disturbance was immediate, and we saw the patient very soon after the beginning of the process and before there were any vitreous opacities, which soon afterward showed themselves. The patient gave a clear specific history and was at once put on appropriate treatment.

Every one probably has his own favorite method of securing rapid mercurialization, as it is so often necessary to do in specific eye troubles. First and most important of all, in my opinion, is inunction persistently employed. From two to eight grams of blue ointment, according to the individual and the severity of the case, should be rubbed in daily; in children one to three grams can be employed daily. A prominent genito-urinary surgeon of New York with whom I have seen cases in consultation, uses as an adjuvant when especially quick results are desirable, the following:

    ℞. Salicylate of mercury....................gr. iii
        Benzoinol ....℥i
    M. Inject ℥ss deep into the gluteal muscles every four days, shaking well first.

Schirmer of Greifswald uses the following:

    ℞. Hydrarg. biniodid .... |25
        Potass. iodid. ....   2|5
        Aq. destil. ....   25|
    M. Sig.: One Pravaz syringeful in the gluteal muscles.

Internally, I am in the habit of giving small doses of calomel (gr. 1/20) every hour, watching the teeth carefully.

Where time is not such an important element, I would still prefer inunction, using less of the ointment and interrupting the treatment from time to time. In specific cases I have accomplished most in the absorption of the vitreous opacities which attend exudative choroiditis by the use of the iodids. As to the subconjunctival injection of solutions of sublimate in these cases I have little experience. I found them painful and not followed

by any surprisingly beneficial results in several cases
of parenchymatous keratitis. The case of choroidal exudation just referred to ran a course of several weeks,
having at the end of this period a large plaque of choroidal atrophy at the macula with a large central scotoma. In a similar case of specific origin I might be
tempted to give the subconjunctival injection of sublimate a trial, hoping that possibly more rapid limita-
tion of the process might be secured. In Deutschmann's
clinic[2] this method was employed in seven cases of so-
called iritis-serosa with exudative deposits on Descemet's membrane, and in twenty-nine cases of choroiditis or irido-choroiditis, and his conclusions were as follows: In three of the iritis-serosa cases the course was
as good as, though no better than, with the usual methods of treatment. In three cases the improvement was so
striking (only three injections about a week apart)
that one could not but ascribe it to the sublimate injections. As to the irido-choroiditis cases, sometimes
the result was negative where a similar negative result
had followed other treatment; in others, again, the injections had a decidedly favorable influence where other
treatment had failed. Deutschmann thinks it is especially indicated in specific eye diseases. The pain following the injection varies, usually lasting two to three
hours, and leaves a conjunctival swelling for one to
eight days, or longer. Usually a 0.1 per cent. sublimate solution (1-1000) is employed, of which 1/10 of a
Pravaz syringeful (i. e., 0.1 m. g. of sublimate) is injected.

Careful investigations by Stuelp[3] and Addario[4] have
demonstrated that these subconjunctival injections of
sublimate could not operate through any bactericidal effect, inasmuch as they did not penetrate into the interior
of the eye in any demonstrable amount. The favorable
results following their use must depend, therefore,
upon the fact that they cause an acceleration of the circulation, especially of the lymphatic circulation. Mel-

linger thinks that the same results would be produced by injecting solutions of salt (¾ per cent.), and his suggestion has been followed by many. Pflüger claims to have found the subconjunctival injection of iodid and chlorid of sodium efficient in cases, 1, of chronic central and peripheric choroiditis, especially the cases of progressive myopia complicated with choroiditis at the posterior pole, frequently localized concentrically about the papilla; 2, in the cases of opacities of the vitreous, usually combined with puncture of the anterior chamber, which increases the effect of the injections.

Schirmer[6] is of the opinion, however, that in recent inflammations sublimate injections accomplish more than the salt solutions.

If the punctate keratitis is not dependent on specific diseases, other treatment may be more satisfactory. Recently a patient came under my observation at the New York Eye and Ear Infirmary, who had been previously under treatment at another institution, where a diagnosis of conjunctivitis had been made. There was, however, no secretion, merely a slight and uniform injection of the whole ocular conjunctiva of both eyes, which almost entirely disappeared on deep pressure, as also after the instillation of a few drops of adrenalin, to soon return, however. The patient, a young married woman, the mother of three children, was in good health and complained of no pain or visual disturbance, but merely of the redness of her eyes. The iris was of normal appearance, the reaction of the pupil normal, as was also the appearance of the fundus, and the vision, with some hyperopia corrected was 20/30. It was thought that it might be a case of vasomotor paresis, and a mydriatic was employed. Then, under these more favorable conditions, my assistant discovered a very few faint spots on Descemet's membrane in both eyes, and the nature of the condition was then apparent. There was a uveitis of both eyes, which, in my experience, is very infrequently met with, especially where it begins in each eye at the same time. There was, no evidence of specific disease, and the patient was put on atropin, ' hot bathing and salicylate of soda, 80 grains a day, with inunctions of mercurial salve, as I do not by any means limit the use of mercurial inunctions to specific cases. Where there is no evidence of specific disease I have generally secured better results with the salicylate of soda in large doses than from the iodids, giving as was suggested by Gifford in sympathetic inflammation,⁶ from 50 to 150 grains a day, according to the severity of the condition.

I recall a patient with a distinct rheumatic history whose vitreous several times became so clouded that it was impossible to see the fundus, but each time cleared up entirely under salicylate of soda. Within a month I have seen a patient, a middle-aged lady, who complained of defective sight in her right eye and very careful examination revealed a very fine haze in the vitreous (vision corrected was 20/40). This patient was gouty and had been under treatment for this condition by her family physician. It seemed most likely that the irritation in the uveal tract might be caused by gout, and I felt warranted in putting her on salicylate of soda.

The etiology of some of these cases is obscure, and they sometimes last a long time and appear to be little influenced by any treatment. In one of my patients, a lady about 45 years of age, the condition started as a keratitis punctata and subsequently there was a fine haze in the vitreous, which lasted for over two years, being sometimes more, sometimes less apparent. She was at the menopause, and it was not impossible that the ocular trouble was in some way associated with the vascular and other disturbances incident to the menstrual irregularity. At no time was her vision less than 20/20, and yet the slight vitreous haze annoyed her excessively. At various times during the two years she was under treatment, I employed the iodids, the salicylates, pilocarpin and other diaphoretics, as well as atropin in the eye, and yet nothing seemed to have much effect in clearing up the vitreous opacities, which gradually faded away after she ceased to menstruate.

The treatment of chronic uveitis in elderly people with more or less marked choroidal changes at the macula and associated often with great visual impairment, has been most unsatisfactory in my hands. I do not remember that I ever saw a case improve under any form of treatment; in fact, the visual impairment of most of the cases I have observed has gradually increased. It has been my usual custom to prescribe iodid of potassium in these cases, but I must confess that I have seen very little, if any, benefit follow its use.

Pflüger, of Bern,[7] contributed recently an article on the subconjunctival injection of hetol or cinnamic acid. He says that Landerer has employed intravenous and gluteal injections of hetol in the treatment of tubercular processes, according to whom it produces a general leucocytosis. An aseptic inflammation about the tubercular foci is caused, leading to the development around and throughout the tubercle first of leucocytes, then of embryonic connective tissue and vessels, and finally of connective tissue encapsulation and to the absorption of the cheesy masses. The histologic changes produced by cinnamic acid injections in tuberculous conditions are, according to Landerer, the same as are observed in the natural healing of tuberculous processes, only they are more active and energetic.

Pflüger endeavored to avail himself of the artificially produced leucocytosis in numerous ocular conditions. He found the hetol injections harmless and unassociated with any ill effects, and claims to have had good results in numerous ocular inflammations. He used a 1 per cent. solution of which he injected 0.4 to 0.5 c.cm. every other day, using massage for a few moments afterward and leaving the eye unbandaged. The pain is inconsiderable and lasts only a few minutes. I have tried it in one or two cases recently. The pain is not considerable,

but it is too soon to tell what are the results. Pflüger
claims to have seen good results from this treatment,
among other conditions, in cases of uveitis of various
etiology and various clinical forms, often with iritis,
or irido-cyclitis serosa as a complication with deposits
on Descemet's membrane. He states that he has seen
severe chronic uveitis combined with diffuse haziness of
the cornea greatly benefited by hetol injections.

I have seldom employed blood-letting except in very
severe forms of iritis, but Fuchs, a man in whom I have
very great confidence, says that in suitable cases blood-
letting is of decided value, using either the natural leech
(5 to 10) or Heurteloup's artificial leech (1 to 2 cylin-
ders full). In inflammation of the conjunctiva, iris or
ciliary body, he takes the blood from the temple, while
in deep inflammation, as in choroiditis, retinitis or neuritis, he advises the blood-letting to be from the mastoid.

There are few cases of uveitis in which atropin is not
indicated as oftentimes also moist heat and at times diaphoresis, as by sweat or hot-air bath, or pilocarpin internally or hypodermically.

Schirmer,[8] in a recent article on the subject of traumatic inflammations of the eye, bears testimony to the
great value of inunction of mercury in traumatic uveitis.
Professor Haab at the Utrecht Congress in 1899, recommended iodoform as an intra-ocular disinfectant. But
to go at greater length into the large subject of the treatment of traumatic or post-operative uveitis would carry
us far beyond the limits of this paper.

To recapitulate briefly it may be said:

1.   That the etiology of the ocular inflammation is
to be investigated in order to obtain some general therapeutic indication.

2.   That in general in acute processes of specific origin,
mercury, best by inunctions, is indicated, aided, if necessary for the absorption of exudates by iodids.

3.   That mercurials are often of service even where
there is no specific cause demonstrable but that

here oftentimes salicylates accomplish more than the iodids.

4. That atropin is pretty generally indicated, aided, if necessary, in severe inflammations by moist heat and diaphoresis.

5. That subconjunctival injections either of sublimate or chlorid of sodium may sometimes be tried. They can do no harm, though it is not yet certain how much good they accomplish or just what are their indications.

BIBLIOGRAPHY.

1. Oph. Review, 1894, p. 259.
2. Deutschmann's Beiträge II, Heft 15, p. 41.
8. Arch. f. Augenh., vol. xxxi, 1895, p. 829.
4. Graefe's Arch., vol. xlviii, 1899, p. 875.
5. Graefe's Arch., llii, 1, p. 42.
6. Trans. Section on Ophthalmology, American Medical Association, 1899, p. 837.
7. Klin. Monatsbl. f. Augenh., 1901, p. 786.
8. Graefe's Arch., llii, 1, p. 1.

DISCUSSION

ON PAPERS OF DRS. DE SCHWEINITZ, WOODS, FRIEDENWALD, HANSELL, WILDER, WOODRUFF AND MARPLE.

DR. GEORGE E. DE SCHWEINITZ, Philadelphia—I would like to emphasize, as my colleague, Dr. Friedenwald, has done, the great importance of investigating the fundus in these cases, for in practically all of them some form of choroiditis can be found. There is one other point, and that is, that where you find descemetitis in association with scleritis and episcleritis, there is pretty sure to be a choroiditis underlying it. I would like to say a word in regard to treatment. I agree with Dr. Marple that the old methods are the best. I have never seen a case in which some good could not be obtained with mercury. I have used subconjunctival injections very much, but have had little result in some cases, but good results in iridocyclitis, always using now the salt solution, having given up the bichlorid. I believe it is the stirring-up of the lymphatic circulation and not the therapeutic action of the drug that produces the beneficial effect. As to the operative treatment, in some cases, where the angle is filled up, operation may do much good in opening it.

DR. JAMES H. SHORTER, Macon, Ga.—Since I moved South I have been struck with the great number of cases of the type Dr. de Schweinitz describes, among negroes, and also its great prevalence among females, and would like to ask Dr. de Schweinitz if they do occur more frequently in females. In a good many of these cases where there was a tendency to constant though intermittent progression, I have often noted a tension as low as minims 2, especially at times of acute exacerbation. At such times the use of atropin did good and brought tension up to normal. There was often an increase of the trouble with each menstrual period. As to the etiology of this disease, I have not been able to find out anything. Syphilis does not seem to be a factor, though so extremely prevalent in the negro race. The prognosis is of the worst. In spite of all treatment the disease always steadily progressed but usually slowly until there was complicated cataract, densely opaque cornea, etc. I tried pilocarpin, iodid of potassium, subconjunctival injections of mercury and other remedies, but no treatment seemed of any value.

DR. J. E. COLBURN, Chicago—I have been struck by the recurrence of certain types of uveitis in the late winter or early spring months and only recently have reviewed a few cases that have been, some of them, for a number of years, under my observation, and where I could predict the return of the patient about March or April with a recurrence of the disease. In this class of cases I have usually found that the elimination by the kidneys is extremely low; that the urine will pass over week after week without varying much from 1008 or 1010 and in which the solids and uric acid are extremely low. Sometimes there is a slight suggestion of albumin and mucin and yet the whole picture is of functional albuminuria rather than structural. I have often had to have them seek a more salubrious and temperate climate; some of them have gone. South and to California and have had but slight attacks and some no recurrence of the attacks. I have found it well to use some aid in elimination—the Turkish bath, salicylate of sodium or strontium and mercurials, and they will often pass over the spring months without a recurrence of the attack. Within a few weeks I saw a patient that I have had under observation for ten years, a woman, who came to me with a very serious condition, her vision being 2/200 in each eye. Almost without exception she has had a return of the trouble during the latter part of each winter. I was surprised on one occasion to find that the irides were attached to the lens at the lower outer segments, and she had well-defined triangular markings in the anterior chambers. The patient has been pronounced free from any organic disease. I saw her this spring with lowered vision, but hope to relieve her condition by the use of eliminants.

DR. LEARTUS CONNOR, Detroit—In the more marked cases of these conditions it has occurred to me to secure results that were very pleasant to the patient by the administration of potassium or sodium iodid, preferably the latter, beginning with very small doses and systematically increasing them, giving it in milk and increasing one grain a day, with an occasional sweat or purge, the doses being increased until they are very large, even in feeble people. Under this treatment the general condition as well as the local condition of the eye improves. A very essential thing is not to give a big dose to start with and it is well to write down on a blank the method of increasing so that there will be no mistake. If the condition of nutrition does not improve then, of course, the remedy is contra-indicated, but I have not found a case in which it did not improve.

DR. E. J. GARDINER, Chicago—I use the iodid of potash in the manner described by Dr. Connor and get very good results. I would like to call attention to the detail in the management of these cases, that has not been mentioned—exercise in the open air with the eyes properly protected, regular exercise in the form of walking I have found very helpful.

DR. HIRAM WOODS, Baltimore—In answer to Dr. Shorter's question about sex, Griffith's cases were confined almost entirely to young females. The majority of my patients were females, the primary attack coming during the second decade of life. I agree with Dr. Woodruff as to the use of pilocarpin. I put the patient to bed, administer pilocarpin for diaphoresis and follow it up with salicylate of sodium, or where I find syphilis, mercury. In reference to the use of atropin, mentioned by Dr. Marple, I would like to ask him if he thinks there are contra-indications for its use. If so, what are they? I have never seen increase of tension in these cases of plastic choroiditis, and always feel safer when the pupil is dilated. The tendency to extend forward is great.

DR. W. B. MARPLE, New York—I think Dr. Woods must have misunderstood me. I did not mean to say that I knew of cases where atropin was contra-indicated, but simply that there may be acute cases of uveitis where it is not indicated. I almost invariably use it and consider it indicated.